BOLAHUN:

An African Adventure

BOLAHUN:

An African Adventure

by Werner Junge, M.D.

TRANSLATED BY BASIL CREIGHTON

ILLUSTRATED

G. P. Putnam's Sons   New York

To my faithful companion

MY WIFE

Contents

Twenty-one illustrations will be found following
pages 56 and 120

BOLAHUN:

An African Adventure

Beyond Civilization

"No, SIGNORE, I am afraid you cannot go on board today. Your boat has suffered damage in the Strait of Messina and will not be here for eleven days. So she will be unable to sail for West Africa before then. The Company deeply regrets the unavoidable delay, but I dare say, sir, you will not mind having to spend a few days in lovely Genoa."

The Italian representative of the Lloyd-Triestino at first wore a look of polite regret, but as he spoke he ran through the whole gamut of facial expressiveness until he finally came to rest in a very meaning smile.

But I was not as delighted by his news as he seemed to expect. What was I to live on during these eleven days now that I had got rid of all superfluous cash in the belief that I was leaving immediately for Africa?

I had to have money, and so I started negotiations, conducted heatedly in two broken languages and ending half an hour later in the offer of financial compensation for the delay. But I was made to feel that if the Company went broke it would be all my fault. "And, of course, if we do go so far, it must be for the class of hotel where you are now staying." That was his trump card, but it failed to take the trick. I was not, as he thought, putting up at a second-rate hotel. On the contrary, I was at quite the most expensive hotel in Genoa, feeling that I might as well enjoy my last days in Europe. Silent and broken, reduced almost to despair, he thereupon paid out my

3

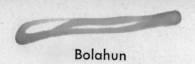

princely subsistence for all the eleven days, and as I took leave of him it was my turn to wear the meaning smile.

Before many hours had passed, however, I was with him again, accompanied this time by Miss Jutta Kolbe, my laboratory assistant, who had meanwhile arrived in Genoa, and with whom I was to continue my voyage. Once more the poor man had to dip into his till and pay out for Miss Kolbe at the same rate. A deeply aggrieved nobleman could not have done it with a lordlier air.

And so we both spent a delightful fortnight at the expense of the Lloyd-Triestino on the sunny, palm-fringed French and Italian Riviera instead of setting out for West Africa. I was going there to take charge of a hospital far away upcountry in Liberia for monks of the Holy Cross, an American Episcopalian order.

My companion, Jutta Kolbe, was a distant acquaintance of my family's, and we had met by chance on a railway platform at Christmas time in 1930. She had just come on leave from Africa, and she told me that the hospital in the tropical forest of Liberia where she had charge of the laboratory was looking out for a doctor. I sent in my name and to my surprise was at once accepted.

Now, a few months later, we met again, but instead of proceeding to Africa we were held up for two weeks on the Riviera, not of our own choice or at our own expense. Not a very promising curtain raiser for a great undertaking!

At last we were on board our boat and steaming once more along that lovely coast to Marseilles, on down the Spanish coast, past the Rock of Gibraltar—which I was to see again nearly ten years later with very different feelings—over the rolling waves of the Atlantic to the Canaries and then to Africa.

As my goal was the interior of Liberia, where its northwest

4

corner extends behind the English colony of Sierra Leone, it suited us better to land at Freetown, the capital of Sierra Leone, than to continue our voyage to Monrovia, the capital of Liberia.

The two days we spent in Freetown, which has a distant resemblance to the towns of the Riviera, were occupied with shopping and making arrangements, after which everything was ready for our return journey into the heart of Africa. Nearly all the Germans of Freetown assembled to see us off. A large completely empty compartment without seats had been reserved for us in the narrow-gauge train bound for the interior of Sierra Leone, and we made ourselves comfortable with deck chairs and basket chairs and such luggage as we needed on the journey.

Late in the afternoon of the first day the train stopped at Bo. Everyone got out and went in search of quarters for the night. We spent the night in the station resthouse. Next morning passengers and train crew were punctually in their places and the journey was resumed. Well, why shouldn't things be done in this way? Notions of time are not the same in Africa as in Europe. Owing to the unavoidable delay at Genoa I was taking up my post about eleven days late. It would never occur to anyone in Africa to waste a word over that. One delay is merely balanced by another. But the astounding thing is that it works, and works without the fever and the fret of Europe.

The second day of our journey resembled the first. By degrees the African scene, the ever-repeated landscape of palms, lianas, jungle grass, and jungle, became wearisome. At station after station there were the same crowds of natives scrambling in and out of the train, offering fruit for sale, and staring at us in astonishment. All this became monotonous. I

5

was therefore thoroughly relieved when we reached the terminus, Pendembu, in the afternoon. There we were loaded with all our luggage on to a truck and driven at the risk of our necks to Kailahun.

Next morning we continued our journey on foot with a train of porters along narrow, winding bush trails, and I suddenly had the feeling that we had plunged into a mysterious green ocean. The last traces of civilization were behind us. On every side virgin forest enclosed us as though we were imprisoned in its impenetrable depths. We were released from all that had hitherto been a necessary part of life, from all the little resources which the world we had known took for granted. We relied now on ourselves, our own strength, our own knowledge, and our own powers. That is one of the chief reasons, as I was to learn years later, why a man who has once lived in the tropics finds it hard to put up with the narrowness of European life. In Africa a man can give his knowledge and capacities full scope; Nature and his environment challenge his utmost exertions, whereas in Europe, and above all in overpopulated Germany, he has to waste his energy in a battle with restrictions and regulations and meaningless details, which are the inevitable consequence of the crowding together of millions of human beings. To put it in a nutshell—in Africa your utmost strength is not enough to exhaust all the possibilities of life; in Europe your strength is exhausted before it is possible to live at all. A man of sound instincts, with the capacity and the strength to get things done, will always feel drawn to go where all his powers will be called upon. Such an opportunity is still offered in the wilds of Africa, which we were that morning getting to know in their primitive state.

A long train of native porters led the way, carrying our trunks and cases on their heads. Next came Jutta Kolbe in a

hammock suspended from long poles and carried by four
natives. The ends of the poles were joined by crossbars, and
these distributed the weight between the four woolly pates.
I brought up the rear in another hammock.

At times our way led through elephant grass six or eight feet
high, at times through dense tropical forest of mighty timber,
lianas, and undergrowth. The natives waded across the small
streams, and if we did not happen to be in our hammocks they
carried us over on their backs. When on these occasions I tried
out the only native words I knew—*"Isser ho"* ("Thank you")
—I thought they would die of laughing—not that they seemed
to need any excuse for laughing among themselves, for they
were doing so most of the time. The word *"loketa"* came in
again and again. I soon discovered that this was their version
of the word "doctor," since they found a difficulty in pronounc-
ing the letters *d* and *r*. As soon as we arrived in a village the
whole caravan would break into shouts of "We're bringing the
doctor," "Here's the doctor," and so on, whereupon the whole
village would turn out in amazement, shaking me by both
hands or catching hold of me in some way or other.

After a march of some hours we suddenly emerged from the
thickly wooded country onto a large open plain, where several
houses stood by the side of the road and a flagstaff was flying
the Liberian flag. This was the frontier station. We now entered the territory of the free Negro republic of Liberia. The
black customs officer reclining in a hammock outside his house
was very obliging and had already let our whole baggage train
pass on ahead of us.

It was now only a short distance to Foya, the first decent-
sized place in Liberia, where we were to change porters and
have a few days' rest. It was here that our first ceremonial
greeting by an important chief took place.

7

Bolahun

As I was sitting in the so-called palaver house, a building in the native style open on all four sides, busily looking over the contents of the provision chest, the Chief Bumbe, or, to give him his battle name, Kukuli, appeared with a numerous escort. He was a well-made, rather stout Negro of about fifty-five, and he came forward with dignity. His head was clean-shaven except at the back, where on the left side a single tuft, in which were woven several small indefinable "charms" about the size of a nut, hung over his left ear like the tip of a nightcap. His beard had been allowed to grow on a circular spot on the left side of his chin, and was twisted to a point an inch or so long. His right eye was disfigured by an old scar, and this gave his lively face a sly and rather villainous expression. He was clothed only in a wide garment of native weave which came up high over both shoulders. His waist was encircled by a cheap and gaudy sash of European manufacture. His dress might not suggest his high standing, but the genuine dignity of his bearing, and the awe with which room was made for him, left no doubt as to who my visitor was. I got up and went to meet him, extending the first and middle fingers of my right hand. He grasped my fingers with the same two fingers of his own right hand and twice we snapped our fingers together with an audible report. I had been practicing this West African brand of the handshake for several days, and at least, I contrived not to disgrace myself. At the same time he greeted me with the word *"Isser,"* which this time had the meaning more or less of "Good day." Good manners enjoin that one shall not immediately respond with *"Isser,"* not until one has gratefully mumbled *"M-m-m"* to show that the whole substance of the greeting has been fully digested. After this short pause the due return of *"Isser"* may be made, whereupon it is greeted on the other side with a grateful *"M-m-m."* These exchanges are repeated several times.

8

The native language lacks the polite flourishes with which we are accustomed to adorn such occasions, and so the people express the cordiality and sincerity of their greetings by frequent repetition and lengthy pauses for digestion.

Meanwhile the chief had sat down on a little carved stool which one of his retinue had placed for him, and he brought this monotonous interchange to an end at last with the question *"Atju kente?"* ("Are you well?") Of course, I had to have this translated, whereupon he remarked that this must be my first visit to his country. If I would remain with him, the whole of his town should be mine; he was just reaching the age at which his father had died, and he would like to have a doctor always at hand. I regretted, I said, that my engagements made it impossible for me to do as he wished, but I assured him nevertheless that my skill would always be at his disposal, and I added that I rejoiced at his being the first to offer me so cordial a welcome to Liberia.

While this lofty diplomatic conversation was in progress about forty pounds of rice were brought in and also a goat on a cord, struggling and bleating piteously. Both goat and rice were presented to me as guest offerings, and custom enjoined that I should take formal possession by touching them. Thanking him heartily, I then offered my presents in return—ten shillings and my last bottle of beer, which unfortunately stood in full view on the edge of the provision chest, and had attracted his Majesty's enraptured gaze throughout our conversation. When I say "offered" I give a very poor idea of what occurred. The actual procedure was that I handed over the money and the bottle to my interpreter, who placed them in the hands of one of the chief's officers, the so-called Speaker. The Speaker then laid them at Bumbe's feet, and he by briefly touching both the coins and the bottle took possession. Then he stood up; we

9

repeated our finger snapping, and the repetitions both of *"Isser,"* which now meant something like *"Au revoir,"* and of the grateful mumbles; and then he retired with measured tread to his own house, leaving me quite exhausted by my first experience of affairs of state. I had also been relieved of ten shillings and my last bottle of beer, but I was richer by a load of rice and a refractory goat. What to do with the goat during the rest of our journey I hardly knew, but I decided that I must have a porter to carry her on his shoulders with her legs tied, and another man for the rice. As the same events occurred, though more briefly, in every village we passed through I soon had to recruit more and more "gift carriers." I began to be afraid I might arrive at Bolahun with a whole herd of goats, but fortunately the smaller chiefs made less magnificent presents, such as hens, eggs, fruit, cola nuts, and rice.

At the end of our last stage, after it had got so dark that our men had to light the way with piassava torches, we were caught by a brief but violent cloudburst which in two minutes soaked us to the skin. Soon afterward a great outcry arose from the head of the caravan and quickly spread to us at the rear. Everybody shouted and yelled, and there were answering shouts from the darkness ahead. We had reached Bolahun. On all sides people loomed up from the dark, and there were great handshakings and much clamor and excitement. Last of all came a white figure with a black cross on his chest, who greeted me with "Hello, Doctor!" I was at the end of my journey.

The extreme northwestern tip of Liberia—the part of it which reaches farthest into the interior of Africa—is bordered on the west by Sierra Leone, on the north and east by French Guinea. It is separated from the coastal region, where the most populous settlements of Liberia and the capital, Monrovia, are situated, by over sixty miles of virgin forest, through which at that time there was no road, so that the chief means of communication with the rest of the world was the railway through Sierra Leone by which I had traveled.

From the summit of Bakufossa, the central and highest point of the whole district, rising far above the forest level, you can view the whole country. Far and wide not a road, not a factory, not a town is to be seen—nothing but endless hills and forest. Here and there you catch a glimpse of a little Negro village half hidden in the jungle; otherwise nothing but trees, endless palm trees, and among them the occasional green patches of rice fields. As soon as you come down from the mountain you are submerged once more in the green sea of leaves. Occasionally you may come on a clearing in the forest where for a short distance you have an open view.

The country is occupied by various Negro tribes whose territories partly overlap the international boundaries. The oldest, poorest, and most primitive are the Giszis. They live crowded together in the least fertile region, wedged in between the Mendis, Gbandis, and Buszis, or Lorma. All of them belong to the great family of the Mandingos, who live on the plateau lying to the north in French Guinea. At the northern tip of the closed territory of the Gbandis, where the great and warlike tribe of Buszis adjoins that of the Giszis and Gbandis, there is a level clearing fifty or sixty yards square which has been trodden hard and smooth for centuries by thousands of naked feet. Here the neighboring tribes bring their produce once a week for sale and barter. From olden days public order has been observed in the market, and the place is holy. Close to this hub of tribal life, yet far enough away to be undisturbed by the lively trafficking and the clamor which seems to be its indispensable accompaniment, the monks of the Holy Cross

11

have their mission-station, Bolahun. On the summit of a low hill is a one-storied building, with a coating of white cement and a gabled roof of corrugated iron, significantly painted with a large black cross. This is the monastery, and from here one overlooks the native dwellings of the pupils and their teachers, the school itself, offices and outbuildings, and, on a small mound, the church, built of hand-sawed rafters and planks. A narrow path leads past a primitive carpenter's shop to the doctor's house and ends a hundred and fifty yards farther on at the convent. Between this and the doctor's house stand the hospital buildings, surrounded by a hedge; and beyond, on every side of the settlement, the untamed primeval forest surges up. The whole area of the mission-station was not a mile long or half a mile wide—a tiny island of civilization lost in the endless green ocean of primeval forest.

Only a few Europeans, moved by unshakable faith in their callings, ventured to leave their own world behind them and press on into a world unknown and interminable, where the forest never released its suffocating pressure, where the climate was deadly, and where they faced the ignorance and dislike of utterly alien and primitive people, not to mention the hostility of thousands of evil spirits, who, according to the beliefs of the natives, lay in wait behind every tree. The aim of these Europeans was not just self-realization; it was more. It was to conquer. They meant to be a nucleus round which helpless and fear-stricken human beings might, as it were, coagulate and crystallize, and also to be a light to lighten that darkness which since time began has brooded beneath the dense forest roof of this part of Liberia.

The four monks were Americans belonging to the Episcopal Church, the five nuns were English Anglo-Catholics, and we two were German Lutherans. It seems scarcely credible today that we lived together on the best of terms in spite of the differences in nationality and creed. In practice, however, differences were so unimportant in comparison with the task we had undertaken that we utterly forgot them.

It would be quite a mistake to think that the monks and nuns were always on the lookout for converts. The toleration and reserve in religious matters, which are inborn and taken for granted among the natives, laid an obligation on the missionaries to turn only to those who first turned to them. The medical attention provided by the hospital and the instruction given by the school attracted many who clung to native superstitions or to the Mohammedan faith; but the door was open for those who knocked and wished to enter. The story of the Gospel told by the missionaries, the example of those who followed the light, and the increase of knowledge and health were the apostles which went from mouth to mouth through the country and made known to the heathen the way to Bolahun. Only a fraction of those who came were baptized as Christians and became Christian missionaries in their turn, but those who took back a spark of the Christian faith and the Christian point of view to their villages are beyond counting. Spark after spark was struck in this way, and the hope and aim of the whole Mission was that from all these many sparks a bright light would blaze out.

It is, of course, obvious that the Church must, if she is to be understood by the minds of primitive men, make certain concessions in outward form, just as the missionaries who once taught us Europeans did in their day. I need only mention the identification of Christmas with the festival of the winter solstice. So, too, one must not judge a church service in the African forest by customary standards. Sunday service in the little timber church of Bolahun, provided only with bare wooden

13

benches, was a surprising scene. The monks were seated near the altar; in the front rows, in clean white shirts and trousers, were the Christian pupils. Behind them every bench was closely packed with Negroes in their best Sunday clothes, men on the right, women on the left. Dogs ran here and there, barking and playing until they were turned out. Some members of the congregation left as fresh ones came in; children carried in slings on their mothers' naked backs babbled, while others were hushed into silence. The sermon of the white father, repeated in a running translation in two Negro languages, was strictly suited to the Negro mind and was followed with the closest attention. As soon as the sermon was over, there was much stretching of both arms over the head, loud yawns and heavy sighs, and at the end of the service the congregation forgathered at the church door, shook hands all round, and gossiped over the events of the past week.

It is absurd to ask anyone to abandon his own personality and at once become what you yourself are or might be. Further, it must not be thought that the Negro has nothing to lose or everything to gain. In the course of centuries he too has become a person with a character of his own. He has, like us, his soul, his personality, and his own moral and philosophical conceptions which have grown with his own growth. It must be clear to anyone capable of reflection that these cannot be the same as ours. But to look on the primitive savage simply as an animal, as is sometimes done—as though his life were expressed simply in the reflex action of instinct—shows a shocking poverty of mind which puts the superior European on a level far below the primitive savage. Human psychology is admittedly a matter of great complexity, but not even to attempt to arrive at any understanding of the Negro for that reason is to commit a dangerous sin of omission.

14

Toleration assumes understanding of the peculiarities of one's neighbor, and understanding again demands at the very least some effort to know what his psychological reactions are. Instead of that, the fate of the whole human race is decided by the rule, as stupid as it is conceited, that anyone who does not resemble me in act and thought is either a fool or a knave; anyone who is not of my faith is a heretic; anyone who does not follow my moral code is immoral; and anyone who does not subscribe to my political views is my enemy and must be destroyed.

I am not going to pretend that I was myself entirely free from this mental attitude when I first found myself among Negroes. On the contrary, I was positively proud of my decided opinions and was glad to have them corroborated by various white sahibs on the coast and inland. I learned that both for the drinking of whisky and for the appreciation of the natives there were cast-iron rules which long experience had tested. During his first spell (European leave comes round every eighteen months in West Africa) the greenhorn pours whisky into his glass to the depth of a matchbox lying flat and fills up with soda water. He also takes all Negroes for angels. On his second trip he measures whisky by a matchbox standing on end, and at the same time, being now a white man who has no illusions, he knows that all natives are rotters and scoundrels. On his third spell he has at last, as an old African, reached the truth on both points; soda water is a superfluous accompaniment of whisky, and the Negro is neither an angel nor a scoundrel but merely a domesticated ape. The black man, a phenomenon of the forest with no personality whatever of his own, has to take his high and mighty European overlord on trust with all his lights and shades; and so the European, if he is wise, adopts this point of view at the outset without falling into either of the initial extremes. The riddle of the native's soul is thus solved.

For a doctor to take such a point of view, however, is unthinkable. The deepest roots of so many ills are in the mind and soul of a sick person, so that a doctor must understand his patient if he means to bring about a cure. He need not be a professional psychiatrist; he must simply put his ear close to the hearts of his fellow men. Nor is this difficult in the case of the Negro, for in spite of his reserve he reveals himself more openly to the inquiring eye, once his confidence is won, than the unreserved European does. It is also far easier to find the way into the soul of the native than it is to penetrate the labyrinthine psyche of the Western man of today.

The uncontaminated "savage" of the Liberian hinterland lives in practice in the early iron age of pre-Hallstatt man. The odd part of it is seen when in the coastal regions this primitive "savage" is abruptly confronted not so much with a three-thousand-year-old culture as with its final outcome, civilization. This collision has deeply affected the disposition and outlook of these now no longer primitive people. A new Negro-soul is coming into existence. It has not yet reached maturity, and it will not be discussed in these pages.

What I am concerned with here are the spontaneous reactions of the uncontaminated "savage" whose acquaintance I made in the Liberian forest.

Ever since Heraclitus the view of the world or of nature which we ourselves have adopted may, perhaps, be described as dynamic, in the sense that our ultimate attempts to explain the universe always rest on a *primum mobile*. The Negro's explanation is magic. With us all is resolved in movement. The very universe moves; the fixed stars themselves are not fixed; electricity flows in a current; light and sound are launched in waves, and electrons circle round a nucleus. In short, movement by dynamic force is the fundamental basis of our living and being. With the Negro all is at rest, and all is bound with all in a magic circle. Everyone is the possessor of a share of this magic power, but he can only exert it and wrest it from the magic circle and bend it to his will by a stronger magic still.

The question "why" and the search for the ultimate cause, which torment us, do not exist for the Negro. Things exist, and what happens happens, by the laws of magic.

A proof of this is to be seen in the composure with which the Negro accepts our latest technical exploits, instead of being thrown, as we expect, into utter astonishment. Why the airplane flies is no problem. It flies by the white man's magic. Technical explanations are wasted on him. He will merely reply, "If I made it it still would not fly." By which he means that he is not in possession of the magic of flight. If he is asked, "Don't the birds fly too?" he will dismiss the question with a smile. He does not understand the question, because for him it is not a question. We on our side do not comprehend the magic powers of faith and will which the Negro has hidden within him and which are so far-reaching that he may die of nothing but the unshakable belief in his death, absurd as this may sound.

Now, since everything is enclosed within the charmed circle of a magic power, it follows that the simplest thing is a carrier of magic and has a magic power. Every object therefore can, if it is enclosed within a circle of higher power than that to which I myself belong, draw me within its magic and so gain power over me. So I must be always on my guard against unknown powers. I must take care to protect myself by still stronger magic. Talismans, taboos, charms, so-called "medicine," awe of the unknown, and all we mean by superstition derive from this. And it explains the power exercised by the medicineman, the witchdoctor. He belongs to a magic power-circuit far beyond the reach of the ordinary man.

The soul of the native of Liberia and all he thinks and does are dominated by this metaphysic. It is the source of his strong religious feeling, of his susceptibility to suggestion, of his attitude to sickness and accident, to law and prohibitions, of his fondness for secret societies and sacrifices, of his ritual practices and moral conceptions; it is, in short, the source of his whole personality.

It seems entirely logical also that the quality which unfortunately is so rare among ourselves—tolerance towards those who think and believe otherwise than we do—should be so strongly developed in the primitive Negro. There have certainly been plenty of feuds and wars among them. There were wars for the acquisition of land, or salt, or slaves; but it has never entered their heads to go to war over religion or ideologies. They would think it absurd to persecute, deride, or abuse anyone for his beliefs, his opinions, or his magic. I knew a chief's family in which the father was a strict Mohammedan, the mother a devout believer in the fetish-worship of her forefathers, and the eldest son a Christian and a pupil of the mission school. All three lived together in perfect harmony and took a sympathetic part by turns in one another's religious ceremonies.

Another matter on which Europeans and Africans often fail to see eye to eye is the quality of patience. The European brings his restless impatience with him into the tropics, and his continual urge to get a move on collides with the unalterable composure and patience of the native. He charges this wall with the fury of a fanatic, only to find that the Negro suffers his heated outbursts with angelic patience, but without responding as desired. The native can never understand this perpetual restlessness and impatient striving to reach some set aim which mark the European.

It is true, of course, that the Negro is "lazy," but the truth is even clearer if that word is first cleared of the reproach we attach to it. Even we put some limits to our lust for work, and his limits are not the same as ours. For him work is not an end in itself. He works for food. He is innocent of any ambition to do more. Besides, he has so little opportunity of improving his position that it seems to him pointless to do a lot more work for a very small return.

Further, it must be borne in mind that the Negro, unless he belongs to a race of merchants or herdsmen, has for generations been a seasonal worker. He is used to hard and heavy work during the planting time of two or three months, after which he is idle again while he waits to gather in the fruits of his labor. This rhythm of alternate labor and idleness is in his blood even today. He throws himself into his two or three months' task and then slacks off. He has done his job, and now he rests, as all his forefathers have done before him. If he has laid up store he often goes so far as to give up his allotment and to "sit down," as he calls it. Nothing but hunger will induce him to work again.

The climate, too, directly invites such a system of life. There is no winter for which forethought must be taken. The heat impairs energy and curbs enterprise, and the luxuriant growth of fruits and grains in most parts of Africa induces a negligent feeling to the struggle of life, particularly when the Negro has not yet had superfluous needs foisted on him by European influence.

For all these reasons he is disposed to regard work as an evil of very limited necessity. We Europeans, who have driven the black man from his paradise, have no right to reproach him with being lazy.

Two other reproaches can be lodged against him with better justification—that he lies and steals. But if you have once understood the train of reasoning which leads him to it you will be able to find some excuse for him. For him it is quite a simple matter: lying is a weapon of the spirit, a rhetorical resource, just as poisoned arrows are weapons of war and of the chase. No one who finds himself in a tight corner will forego a good weapon. After all, is an atom bomb more moral than a lie? Or can that morality which condemns a lie and approves the saying that the end justifies the means boast of any superiority? Stealing, on the other hand, is condemned by the black man as by us, owing to his wholehearted respect for property. But almost every European is a nabob in his eyes. And so, he concludes, a trifle here and there, a few cigarettes or a shilling or two, will never be missed. Indeed, we are thought petty or miserly if we make a fuss.

When we come, however, to the love of one's neighbor, the native reveals such a total lack of any such feeling that, used though we are to our frequent compromises with this noble ideal, his inhumanity shocks us again and again. If an aged or weakly person falls by the way and is attacked by ants, a Negro will leave him to his horrible fate without a tremor. I have often and often had the greatest difficulty in protecting a sick person who was creeping to me on all fours for help from the risk of being beaten or stoned. The dread of getting caught up into the ill-omened circle of this unfortunate man was stronger than any stirring of human feeling, pity, or neighborly love. In such moments I saw very clearly what a tremendous task it was for the first time in such a world as this to preach the doctrine of love between man and man, because, just as we cannot imagine a

20

world utterly devoid of any feeling of neighborly love—which has become second nature to us—so the primitive Negro cannot imagine a world in which he is expected to exercise charity without any thought of reward.

In one respect, however, the natives are very much our betters, although they are often unjustly blamed on this very point because their clothing leaves them partly naked; yet their sense of decency is spontaneous and genuine to a degree scarcely found nowadays among us. Shame with them is deeply engrained and confined strictly to the primary aspect of sex. If a party of men, emerging from the forest, comes upon some women bathing in the river, screaming and laughing as they do on almost every occasion, the men shout a warning in advance, and the women submerge to the waist. The men ford the stream with a little innocent chaff, but do not look in their direction. Everything to do with sexual life and feeling is treated in a perfectly natural way and as a means to the wished-for aim of reproduction. To thwart this aim by artificial means is inconceivable to them. Indeed, according to their notion of living again in their children, it is suicide. Their polygamy, too, so much inveighed against, is not the result of sexuality, but is simply the best solution, as things are, of a social problem. Polygamy is merely the consequence of the proportion of men to women (1 to 1.8 upcountry in Liberia), of the high rate of infantile mortality, of the high percentage of sterile women, and of the shortage of cheap labor.

When overzealous missionaries in the interests of modesty cover up the women's naked bodies I can only smile, but when they succeed in their campaign against polygamy I feel the deepest distress. They reopen social problems for which they have no better solution to offer, and by their ceaseless striving to do good they bring their own efforts to confusion and the people they meddle with to misery and destitution.

When I saw how close to nature the instincts of the Negro were, I realized how utterly the European has renounced his inborn faculties. The forest is like an ocean. We Europeans are soon lost in it unless we rely on a compass; yet the native can find his way with unerring certainty. He scents game, feels the coming storm, divines the approach of harm and the threat of danger. He can no more explain all this than we can understand it. One day one of my boys came to me and asked for leave because his mother had called to him. His mother lived eighty miles away. He had had no news of her, but he heard her call. He returned two or three weeks later and told me that he had found his mother still alive, but that she died a few days after his arrival. I knew this boy well enough to know that he was telling the truth. I have never been able to understand it. But I do know that we Europeans, in our progress away from nature and from the soul of the savage, have also fallen a long way behind in our instinctive reactions.

Considering how dubious we may well feel of the correctness of our own views of life, we have no right, it seems to me, to look down with contempt on the savage. Would it not be better to pocket our pride and to recognize that we and they are human beings who, after going our separate ways for thousands of years, have suddenly come face to face again? Now we regard each other distrustfully, talk at cross-purposes, and don't understand each other.

In my present task, too, all depended on the wish for mutual understanding and on the pains taken to acquire it. There is no other way of bridging the gap between the Negro of the primeval forest and the civilized European.

CHAPTER 2

The Hospital in the Forest

I BEGAN my first morning in my new home with a tour of the hospital, which had the fine name of St. Joseph's. Taking the African forest into account, it was a thoroughly creditable institution, and although it consisted only of several one-storied buildings, partly in the native style, partly of wood, and partly of sun-dried bricks, it contained in the simplest form all the strictly necessary equipment of a tropical hospital.

As assistants I had first of all Jutta Kolbe, who was experienced in the work of a laboratory and also familiar with the running of the place. In addition, there were the nurses. These nurses were all men, since the native women were as unfit for hospital work or the dressing of wounds as for any other cooperation with Europeans, which requires a certain degree of intelligence or adaptability. I do not mean that the fair sex among them has a prescriptive right to stupidity. In later years I have received a great deal of welcome help from black women, but owing to her place in society the woman of the primitive forest tribes is wholly inhibited from taking up any unfamiliar work.

The rest of my hospital staff was composed of seven natives. The most important of them was James Njuma, a young Giszi. He was the only one of the native contingent who could read and write. He was extremely capable in every way, an excellent assistant who even carried out minor operations on his own, in which he was helped by speaking several languages, no small

23

advantage considering the number of different races and languages represented. He was my right-hand man and bore the proud title of house surgeon.

After him came Joseph Ngombu, the son of an important Mendi chief. He could at least read and write figures and was a master of the great art of taking temperatures. But this went so near to exhausting his mental resources that his colleagues gave him the nickname of Empty Matchbox.

The operating theater was in the charge of a young Giszi named Bokai, while a Gbandi named Mentjo was responsible for applying the dressings. Ndobbo, a Giszi, a very lively fellow and an excellent clown, who was called the Cock because of his Don Juan-like propensities, ruled the outpatients' department. In charge of the baths was old Salifu, and a Buszi, Momo, directed the laundry. In the course of time and as we became busier, others joined the staff, but only Hermann Mukurry calls for special mention. Hermann was a rolling stone, driven by a caprice of fate from his native Cameroons into our forests. As he spoke German, English, French, and Arabic, he was the very man for the post of clerk. To say that he "spoke" is an exaggeration, because he stammered so frightfully that he could never get to the end of a sentence, particularly when he got excited, which, in fact, was all the time. He was only free of this impediment when he sang. But as this means of communication seemed to me too operatic, his intercourse with me was always by writing. A complaint about Njuma, the house surgeon, which I accidently preserved in my diary is given here as an example of our correspondence:

SIR:

I have been here in Bolahun over seven months today without disturbance I believe, therefore I will not have no friend, why? I will not put my foot into the middle. First, I am not a Giszi I believe. Yesterday I heard my name again from Njuma. Therefore I beg you that you will tell him to let my name alone, he likes to mix everyone together that is his way same as he has done with teacher Monle. Today I let it go the next time I will sell myself for money.

HERMANN MUKURRY

By this he meant that Njuma had spread some false report about him, and so he asked me to reprove him, and threatened that the next time he would take action against him for slander.

In addition to these highly qualified assistants there was a varying number of cooks, farm workers, overseers, water carriers, and casual laborers, who were recruited largely from among the patients.

Such were my assistants in coping with the pressure of work; and in order to keep pace with it I had to adopt a program and methods which may perhaps not conform with European ideas. Work began just after dawn, when I went the round of my patients. As Empty Matchbox could read temperatures, but could never learn how to trace the graph, the doctor had to do this on his round. So as he approached a patient's bed, the orderly's voice boomed out with pride: "Temperature 101.5, pulse 80, latrine twice." While I was making my round a solemn tattoo was beaten in front of the outpatients' department on an old iron railway sleeper. At this sound the outpatients turned out.

Every second day was injection day for the large number of patients who had to be treated with bismuth injections. They were drawn up and told off by my house surgeon. The new cases were separated off to be seen by me. The old cases marched away one by one, starting from the left, into the open ward, and showed their "tickets," or numbers, as these were

25

read out in a loud voice by the house surgeon or Hermann. Jutta stood at a desk and ascertained from the entries in the injection book what dose each patient was to have. The next orderly cleansed the prescribed spot with alcohol and a third administered the injection in their buttocks. Rubbing the place, and grinning with delight and confusion, the patients then went out at the other end of the ward. As a rule two nurses injected at the same time, while two others cleansed the syringes at a table, fitted freshly sterilized needles, and refilled the syringes. The whole affair went with a speed scarcely credible in such surroundings; in an hour well over a hundred patients could be dealt with. Yet often during serious outbreaks of sickness injections were given for six hours on end. Meanwhile the new cases were inspected and the treatment prescribed. They then fell in with the main contingent for injections.

Next all stomach and bowel cases among the new patients were told to come forward. Each was given a large piece of fresh banana leaf, taken behind a palm-leaf screen, and told to hand over a specimen to the laboratory for analysis. They then returned to the medical ward with a ticket giving the result of the analysis, the doctor meanwhile having taken charge of injections to relieve the chemical analyst. At the same time all other sufferers from internal complaints came along, having been marshalled by the house surgeon.

After a short midday break the inpatients were given medical attention, and while this went on there was the distribution of medicine in the outpatients' department. All tablets and pills were given daily to the Negroes in daily doses. It was impossible to trust them with a larger quantity because they could not keep the instructions for each dose in their heads. Furthermore, they harbored the strange conviction that aspirin tablets were just as beneficial when bound to the head or arm, and also they devoured ointments at the risk of their lives; and so it was necessary to place each tablet, as issued, straight into each patient's mouth. To be sure it was swallowed a second nurse stood beside the "apothecary" with a bucket of water and a cup, from which each patient had to take a gulp and finally he had to show his empty mouth to a third nurse before he was allowed to go. Unfortunately I seldom had time to look on at this comic scene, for I had had to pass on to the remaining fresh patients from whom blood or urine tests had been required and to any other cases where diagnosis and treatment were still in doubt.

Last of all there was the evening round, with its magic formula "102.6, pulse 100, latrine once." But even then we often sat on by lamplight in the laboratory to carry difficult analyses to their conclusion. Nothing could be left over, since the next day had to be kept free for new tasks.

Every other day, after the morning round in the hospital, was the day for operating, and at the same hour the improvised gong summoned all surgical cases to the outpatients' ward. Cases of tropical ulcers on the leg and other suppurating sores were very numerous. They came on in single file from the left, just as the injection cases did, and put their affected legs up on a long pole running right across the open ward. Behind this pole the nurses stood side by side, and behind them again there were other nurses at a large table, preparing large pieces of lint and ointment and cutting them to the size required. The first nurse behind the pole unwound the patient's bandage and threw it and the dressing into a pail at one side. Then the patient hopped to the next nurse, who cleansed the wound. Now it was the turn of the doctor or his deputy, Njuma, to say what dressing was to be applied to the wound. The next nurse applied the prescribed dressing, and the last did the bandaging. Thus the patient hopped his way right across the building and left it at

27

the other side freshly bandaged. As with the injections, the nurses worked double shifts, so that up to a hundred bandages could be applied in the hour.

The ointments and lotions often had names which the nurses found quite unpronounceable, so they invented names of their own with the same sort of sound. The dressings, which had to be cut to the size of the wound, were for brevity's sake given the sizes of coins; and although the wounds were often larger than the largest English coin, the half crown, the valiant dresser was not at all put out; he merely invented larger ones. An imaginary five-shilling piece was clearly twice the size of a half crown, a ten-shilling piece twice again, and so on. Thus you might hear the house surgeon, Njuma, call out over his shoulder, "A seventeen-and-sixpenny snake ointment" or "£2 palm-oil." I never knew him give a wrong size.

Dubious cases were held over for the doctor after he had come to the end of his three or four operations. Then came the examination of all fresh surgical cases and their treatment. After the midday break, during the routine issue of medicines, and after the daily round of the inpatients, the aseptic dressings, lancings, plaster bandages, and so forth were carried out. Finally, dates were arranged for the more serious surgical operations. When the patient had paid, a day was fixed for taking him into the hospital. He was given as many pebbles as he had days to wait. He threw one pebble away daily and so arrived on the right day.

The week went by according to this alternating curriculum, and we could get through our daily program only by keeping to it strictly. It worked very well apart from the one defect that no allowance was made for unusual occurrences such as accidents and other pressing emergencies, which, after all, must be expected in a hospital. Many a night I used to sink dead tired into my bed and yet be unable to sleep because of the unceasing clatter in my head, "Ticket number 4324, thirteen-shilling snake ointment, and latrine six times."

In the hospital itself there were at first only twenty-eight beds available, and only fifty after the annexes had been built. Only the most serious cases of sickness, therefore, could be taken in besides those surgical cases for whom operations were necessary. For these the beds were usually reserved months in advance; any complicated or protracted clinical treatment put us back and had to be avoided for this reason alone. The number of inpatients never varied throughout the year and we never had vacant beds at Bolahun.

But it was another matter with the outpatients. Their number varied considerably. In the summer months, the rainy season, there was a comparative lull. In the autumn with the end of the rains the number of patients slowly rose until it reached two or three hundred a day, increasing steadily during the dry winter months and reaching its maximum as a rule at New Year and before the beginning of the next rainy season. At this period the daily attendance in the outpatients' department varied from eight hundred to a thousand, and once reached the record number of twelve hundred. At such times it took us all our strength and time to cope with the onset, and we had to appoint additional orderlies, whom we called policemen, to prevent our being overwhelmed. Occasionally we engaged fanga players (the fanga is a sort of lyre) or singers to keep the waiting crowd quiet; and it was at such times too that we had most need of extra interpreters, since the sick often came from a distance. We had them not only from the surrounding tribes of the Gbandis, Giszis, and Buszis, but also Mendis from Sierra Leone, Mandingos from French Guinea, and from Liberia came Gpesses, Golas, and Vais. We had to reckon too with the large number of lone wanderers from even more distant places, so that including those who spoke only French or English we often had a babel of ten or twelve different tongues. Sometimes the translation passed through two interpreters, and the final result had very little resemblance to what had originally been said. In desperate cases they had to fall back with much laughter and shouting on signs, mixed with expressive primitive noises.

As a rule the sick arrived in parties from the same neighborhood, and after waiting for one another returned home again in a body. Serious cases, children, and the aged were taken care of by their relations, so that Bolahun was always inhabited by a large number of healthy persons as well as by all the sick.

The difficult problem of lodging them all had been solved before my time. There was a regular hospital town near the hospital buildings themselves, and there, in palm-leaf huts, the sick and their attendants dwelt under the eye of a chief appointed by the mission for the purpose. These huts, crowded together without plan, were about five feet high, made merely of palm leaves, some of them decayed, some new. The floating population of the settlement, known as Giszitown from the prevalence of Giszis there, ran up to a thousand, but as their residence was brief, they had no desire to do much for those who followed them. The sanitary arrangements were shocking, and the crowding together in such primitive conditions of people suffering from all sorts of diseases inevitably led to the spread of disease, and so the work of the hospital never grew less.

I made up my mind to alter all this and to have a model settlement on hygienic principles. By taking hygienic measures most tropical diseases can be checked just as effectively as European diseases. Ignorance of the simplest measures for the protection of health was the only explanation of the way in which any outbreak of infectious disease among the Negroes grew at once to an epidemic which could be brought to a halt only through a slowly acquired immunity. One of those endemic diseases, by which in particular almost all the Giszis are affected, is the yaws, a disease which takes a course very similar to that of syphilis with us. If there is any contact with a yaw ulcer its germs invade a healthy body through any slight abrasion of the skin. The frequent ulcerations of the legs of Negroes, already mentioned, were often related to the yaws. Diseases due to intestinal worms were of many kinds and very frequent, as were those sicknesses due to worms which live in the tissues outside the intestines and lay their eggs in the blood or externally. Bilharziasis and ringworm infections complete the number of parasite diseases of this sort. Elephantiasis, causing gigantic deformity of the extremities and the organs of sex, is one of the diseases due to worms. Further diseases of a parasitic kind are the numerous cases of amoebic dysentery, malaria—to be dreaded particularly among children—and lastly, though more rarely, sleeping sickness, which as a rule came from French Guinea. Mushroom poisoning, leprosy and diseases due to flymaggots, a special form of scabies, and the complications following on sand flea bites gave a great variety of skin diseases. We had also, with few exceptions, all the long list of ailments familiar in Europe, with the difference that owing to neglect they appeared often in chronic forms. Among other things I saw swelling of the belly or of the extremities which were almost as big as the man himself. Illnesses which had gone on for years and even decades had produced conditions never to be seen even as curiosities in European medical schools.

The reason why so many patients displayed these advanced

and chronic states was partly because doctors were very rare in that part of Africa. Seeing a doctor very often meant a journey on foot lasting weeks and an absence from home running into months. The cost of all this was more than the average Negro could afford. Often his illness prevented his making the journey at all. He could not afford bearers or else could find none who were not afraid to carry him because of his sickness. And so he had no choice but to put off his journey until he was driven to it by pain or desperation. Then he needed weeks for a trip which a man in good health would have made in a few days, and if he got to his journey's end his money was spent and his provisions used up. These unfortunate human beings were to be seen any morning lying about in front of the hospital in a deplorable plight.

And when the sufferer found his way at last to the doctor, the same question always arose: Why did he not come sooner? If only months or years before, he had overcome the difficulties he had now overcome! The answer to this was to be found partly in the Negro's attitude to sickness. According to his philosophy, sickness was a spell which had been put on him. This spell, or decree of fate, had to be accepted or else overcome by a stronger magic. The man of strongest magic was the medicine man. On receipt of certain offerings he performed some hocus-pocus, and if this primitive exorcism did not work, then the magic from which the sick man suffered was stronger than the magic of the medicine man, and there was nothing for it but to put up with the pain and suffering. It was only when he heard that other victims of the same magic had been released by the white medicine man that he thought it worth his while to undertake the wearisome journey. The idea that illnesses were spread by living germs or could be in some way infectious was completely incomprehensible to him. The magic which got one man got another, and the only way to keep well was to overcome this magic. If he had fallen sick the sick man must confess what he had done. Had he trodden upon a charm or taken hold of it and eaten it? Who were his secret enemies? All the many possibilities had to be gone through. It followed logically from this way of thinking that the medicine man who had the magic to counteract such a spell must also have the power to make anybody sick if he chose to. This faith in witchcraft was no help towards curing a patient, but it did at least have the pleasing effect of inspiring respect for the doctor and prompt obedience to his commands. This was challenged only once, when a Mohammedan "colleague" whose business in sorcery was declining owing to my "dirty competition" tried to overcome me by his magic. I found small, tightly bound packets containing texts from the Koran and unidentifiable leaves and so forth under the mat in front of my door, under my chair in hospital, and in my laboratory. To the horror of my black companions I put the things in my trouserpockets and carried them about with me.

These views of the Negro about the nature of his illness called for a special psychological approach on the part of the doctor. Any doctor in Europe is familiar with the patient who is not so much interested in what disease he has got as in how he can have got it. The Negro, as will be clear from what has been said, is not interested in either of these questions. He wants to know only one thing—whether the doctor has the magic for his illness or not. Diagnosis and aetiology have no interest for him; even therapy, the manner and method of the process of healing, is of no interest either. He wants nothing but a precise and binding forecast. A forecast circumscribed by "if" and "but," even though it is accompanied by suitable medical explanations, is to him merely a way of disguising the fact that

33

in his case the requisite magic has not been exercised; for the same reason, he expects the treatment to produce almost instantaneous results. The cure must naturally follow immediately if the injurious sorcery has been overcome. Lengthy treatments, unless they have been clearly announced in advance, are a sign of the weakness of the healing magic. On the other hand, he regards it as obvious that the magic cure must be accompanied by its appropriate commands and prohibitions, which must be obeyed with painful accuracy. Indeed, the stricter these rules and prohibitions are, the stronger is the magic and the firmer his faith in it. It seems to him, too, particularly important that the magical cure shall be linked with some clearly recognizable concomitant phenomenon in which its power is revealed. The more painful the procedure the more effective it must be. For this reason we sometimes administered purgatives at the same time as medicines of slow and unobtrusive effect, so as to establish faith in the cure.

Patients never showed any reluctance or fear over submitting to the measures prescribed for them. Whatever was required was carried out without hesitation and with complete faith. They make ideal patients for a conscientious doctor. But this eagerness to undergo any treatment has its drawbacks. Again and again their desire to have injections and operations instead of merely taking pills and tablets proved almost invincible. They even attempted to reach their goal by deceiving the doctor in his diagnosis, by giving a false history of their complaint or by simulating false symptoms, because they believed that thus they would arrive at injections or an operation. This habit, as well as their erroneous notions of the causes of illnesses, their weakness for boasting, exaggeration, and long-winded tales, and the demands made upon interpreters, induced us in most cases to do without any sort of case history. I even dropped such questions as, "How long has it been hurting you?" after being given the answer, "Ten years," in an early case of appendicitis, and after being told that a recent case of gonorrhea had existed since birth. Even when their intentions were of the best, it was often very difficult to know just what the trouble really was. I remember the case of a boy of twelve or thereabouts who was brought to me because he had not yet begun menstruation. It took me some time before I grasped that in his tribe the bilharziasis worm was endemic, so that all boys of an age to start work in the rice fields were affected with haematuria. The symptom was so universal in the tribe that they took it to be a normal sign of maturity. This boy was a son of the village smith and as he was being taught the trade of his father he had avoided work in the rice fields and the consequent infection. He therefore remained healthy, and so he was brought to me. To attempt to explain all this would have been quite useless. It was simpler to induce the required symptoms by giving a harmless medicine, and father and son went happily home again.

Another time I had a woman patient who, when asked what she complained of, instantly replied, "Nothing." I asked what was the matter, then, and where she felt ill. She gave no answer. But when I asked what she had come for I got the rather injured and indignant reply, "Are you not the man who makes women pregnant?" Then I understood that she had come to be treated for sterility.

I was often left quite in the dark by the answer I was given. "The worm that circles in the body" requires each time a thorough overhaul, since it concealed the most diverse ailments. Also the terse reply, "I have been bewitched," without further explanation, called for careful examination until the evil spell was found to be dysentery, malaria, or pneumonia.

Bolahun

The treatment of the yaws by injection and the instantly successful results were, of course, talked of far and wide; it was very soon the same with surgical successes of the more obvious kind. Consequently the pressure of cases for operating was soon very great. These operations in the tropical forest were, of course, very different in all their circumstances from the same operations in Europe. To start with, the equipment of the operating theater and all the arrangements were naturally primitive. My first concern was to ensure that anything coming directly or indirectly into contact with the incision was completely aseptic. Even that aim encountered unbelievable difficulties. Flies came in at the windows, which were neither glazed nor netted, and alighted everywhere, so that I had to have an extra orderly for fly-control; and over and over again unforeseen accidents interfered with the smooth course of an operation. Once ants invaded the theater and the operation had to be concluded in a sea of petrol. A sudden tornado once compelled us to shut every window, and I had to carry on by the light of hurricane lamps. Once a patient under a local anesthetic declared that he had had enough and wanted to go. It was all we could do to persuade him to lie where he was. Another insisted on turning on his side; he couldn't always lie on his back. My native helpers too gave trouble. The thread ran out in the middle of an operation and had to be fetched from the mission and sterilized, while I stood waiting in a fury. An orderly always had to sit at the patient's head to keep him quiet and talk him out of any of the inappropriate things he might wish to do. A sterilized towel hanging over a hoop made him invisible to the surgeon. Once I heard a loud snore, and discovered that the orderly, instead of composing the patient, had composed himself to sleep with his head on the breast of the long-suffering victim. Another time there was a terrific

crash during an operation. Patient and orderly lay on the floor.
Once more the orderly had fallen asleep on the patient's breast
and in doing so had released the hinge at the back of the top
end of the operating table and brought down the whole affair.

For a time, until the assistants at an operation had reached
the stage of working together in a dependable manner, the
surgeon, while he did his own work, had to keep an eye on
what everybody else was up to. And even later on it was just
as well to be ready for surprises. Owing to the heat I had
arranged for an orderly who was employed on odd jobs in the
theater to wipe the sweat from my face when I told him to.
One day the usual orderly had been relieved by another. At a
difficult moment in the operation I asked him for a sponge.
Whereupon, in this moment of tense concentration, I had my
face well washed with a wet swab.

The first time I used an anesthetic made an extraordinary
impression. The effect on the staff when they saw a patient
under an anesthetic and found later that he remembered nothing whatever of the operation was profound. "First the doctor
kills a man and then he brings him to life again!" "The doctor
can make a man dead without killing him!" It exceeded all
they had ever imagined, and their belief in surgery passed all
limits. A humpback wanted to have his hump removed and
would not be convinced that it could not be done.

The demands made upon me would have very soon exceeded
my utmost capacity, even if I had had the time to meet them;
for after all I had not come to Africa as a fully experienced
surgeon. It was only slowly, step by step, making every effort
to avoid mistakes which would have lain on my conscience
and cost me the trust of my patients, that I was able to venture
from ruptures and appendixes to more serious operations.

37

Even so, I was not, of course, spared some mistakes and failures.

Unpleasant complications were particularly frequent in my first operations on the great swellings due to elephantiasis. Yet there were so many successes that the occasional failures, which always trouble a surgeon more than his successes cheer him, were not taken amiss by the natives. On the contrary, the greater the complications and the more elaborate the treatment, the greater in their eyes was the merit of the achievement. A simple extraction was not so glorious as the tiresome operation of removing a root after the tooth had been broken off.

Once when I was operating on a very large hernia, using a local anesthetic, my patient, a woman, suddenly had a fit of coughing, and then fainted after extruding all her "innards" into my arms. It took me much time and pains to get them back again and sew up the wound. As a reward for my labors she made a perfect recovery without any complications.

I only once completely forfeited the confidence of my patients, and it was precisely when I was free of all blame and had operated for years with success. A woman died of pneumonia a few days after a simple abdominal operation. The natives acknowledged with regret that God had abandoned their doctor, and so they in their turn abandoned the hospital. For days only a few long-standing patients came for treatment, until one day a man turned up who had not heard that God had turned his face from the doctor. I performed on this man a successful operation for elephantiasis, and three days later they all came back, congratulating themselves and me on the restoration of my power, and all was as before.

The utter lack of qualified surgeons far and wide made it necessary that I should perform operations strictly reserved as a rule for the specialist. I was astonished at the speed with which the news traveled that I had performed, for example, my first operation for cataract. In a few days sufferers from cataract came streaming in, and continued to do so until I had some fresh success, and then a new stream set in.

The treatment required after the operation itself was a chapter by itself. For the natives a successful operation was the whole magic, and to wait for the wound to heal was just putting off the happy moment when they could display their cure before the eyes of their family. Their childlike delight when cured was, indeed, the best reward for all a doctor's trouble. I can never forget the moment when a sufferer from elephantiasis was freed of an immense swelling of the scrotum. He had only a spinal anesthetic, and the moment the tumor fell away in the course of the operation he gave a heartfelt shout of joy and could not do enough to express his delight and gratitude. But waiting for the wound to heal was more than he could endure. Also the Negroes thought that their own magic might be better for such a trivial matter, and so they unwound their bandages and laid leaves on the wound or smeared it all over with some obscure concoction. If they were out of pain they got up secretly in the night and sat by the fire to show each other their wounds, and then bandaged them up again "just right" with hands smeared with palm oil from their last meal.

Consequently it was at first extremely difficult to achieve the best results and avoid setbacks. But the high expectations they had of me and their childlike trust forced me to do my very utmost. If anything went wrong a strict investigation followed, and everything was done to eliminate the cause of it.

The hospital buildings themselves, which were no longer equal to the ever-increasing demands made upon them, were one of the chief causes of failure. Very soon, therefore, I began drafting plans for alterations and additions. As there was no skilled labor or European materials to deal with, it was a simple matter to draw up the plans. To find the money required was a great deal more difficult. The funds allotted by the mission to the hospital were naturally limited, and the purchase of medical necessaries pretty well exhausted them. Nevertheless, the monks were enthusiastic.

The extension of the hospital was therefore taken in hand with the full support of the mission. Again and again the work had to be broken off, and it was months before it was all brought to a conclusion. The outpatients' department was moved to the other end of the hospital buildings and the whole hospital faced the other way. This was just as well, because I was all this time planning a further building operation which would have made the change of front necessary in any case. This plan was the removal of the hospital town to a new site. I could not expect any financial help from the mission, as it was already paying for the alterations to the hospital, and so I had no choice but to set about it with what resources the hospital had of its own and with the help of the patients.

The hospital had no actual income of its own. Treatment was free and only the inpatients had to give the hospital some rice in advance for their own consumption. The palm oil and vegetables to go with it, as well as fruit, were supplied from the hospital farm. Meat was only occasionally bought. Normally it does not belong to the native economy, since in Africa it is a rarity. Black people do not eat eggs. On entering the hospital a patient was, as a rule, required to bring twenty pounds of rice; and if a quick turnover of patients was achieved by hastening their discharge, the slowly accumulating stock of rice could be used to pay my workpeople.

Each man took half his wage in rice tickets, the so-called doctor's money, which he could exchange for rice when it suited him. As this doctor's money was independent of the market and did not follow the price of rice, it was very popular and changed hands so rapidly that a quantity of tickets finally vanished and were never presented for payment. Since then I have realized that even a sound currency needs only partial cover.

To obtain a further source of income, which would impose no hardship on my patients and yet be of help to me, I introduced the rule that each sick person coming for treatment should pay two iron pieces, worth one penny, for his card and number. The natives of this part of Liberia, besides the official coinage, the English shilling, had a currency of their own, handed down from their forefathers. It consisted of twisted pieces of iron of the thickness of stout wire, about fifteen inches long and beaten flat at both ends. Twenty of these "irons" were bunched together and had normally the value of a shilling. All payments were made in this coinage. It had the advantage of serving also as a valuable and much coveted raw material, but the great disadvantage of being very unwieldy. For example, if a man wanted to sell a cow in the market for a hundred shillings he needed a small caravan of bearers to carry home the two thousand "irons." I, too, had to have a giant chest made for me as the hospital treasury. It would have needed at least ten or twelve men to move it.

Rice and "irons" were all I disposed of for the building of my town. But, in spite of all I could do, I was unable to raise the money. Clearing the forest, leveling the site, making roads, building the sixty native dwellings I had planned, with palaver house and chief's house, bathhouses and latrines, not to mention the inauguration festivities, cost all told about £145, of which I was able to earn only £115. So I paid the missing £30 out of my own pocket. It was not too much to pay for the high

41

dignity of being the supreme chief of Loketahun (Doctortown), as the natives christened it. Many a man has paid more than that for a title, and the title of Chief of Loketahun, even without the large number of wives to which the holder of such a dignity was entitled, was not to be despised, particularly when it included the great joy of having provided decent housing for some thousands of sick persons.

CHAPTER 3

Fire, Beasts, Epidemic

UNFORTUNATELY the natives of the Liberian forest had no idea of privacy. Considerate and alive to the feeling of shame in their own persons as they were, they set no value on the control of curiosity. When at the end of my day's work I climbed the little hill on which my house stood, children and women, and men too, would be standing or sitting on my veranda lost in amazement at a white man's home. My arrival did not in the least put them out; they could now, through the open windows, enjoy the remarkable sight of me at my supper or at whatever else I might be doing; and they did so too, with many astonished and marveling comments. At last I had to have a fence run around the bottom of the hill to enclose the whole of my land. I also posted an old patient as watchman at my door. Otherwise I should have had no peace.

My house, considering its situation in the African forest, was very comfortable. The grey cement floors and walls made a rather chilly and bare impression, and the furniture to start with was very primitive, but besides the veranda I had a fine large sitting room, a dining room, bedroom, bathroom, and a spare room. None of these rooms, except the spare room, was quite unfurnished; even the bathroom was provided with a bath, which could be filled at need with water, although at other times it stood outside to catch the rain.

A bath is by its very nature an unwielding piece of furniture, and according to an old African saying one can tell how deeply

43

a man has penetrated into Africa by the size and description of his bath if, that is, there is nothing else to go by. On the coast the European takes his bath in a tub with water laid on just as he would at home. Eighty miles inland the hot water tap is sure to be missing, and the bath is one of zinc. A hundred and fifty miles upcountry the bath becomes an oval zinc tub such as is used for the home laundry, and it is filled from a bucket. The size of this vessel diminishes with further penetration into the continent, until presumably it shrinks to the size of a coffee cup. The inconvenience of endeavoring to fold up my seventy-odd inches in a vessel measuring under forty in length induced me to construct a shower bath and to buy as my first personal acquisition an ordinary zinc bath of the largest dimensions. The small one I kept only to take on treks.

As soon as I was done with the new buildings for the hospital, I had proper furniture made for me by a native carpenter. For weeks my free time was taken up with painting my walls and ceilings. Doors and window frames were stained, and finally an American missionary who was very clever with his hands built me a very fine fireplace when he came to pay me a visit. This crowning glory had only one disadvantage— it would not draw properly.

One of the monks made repeated attempts to make this beautiful fireplace draw. He came to the eventual conclusion that certain alterations to the chimney would put it right, and he set to work on it from the roof. When all work in my house had ceased and just as I was proudly showing off my fine abode to the nuns, a leg in a sock and shoe burst suddenly through the roof and put the nuns to flight. After that we abandoned all further attempts, and when we lit the fire just let it smoke. At first the smoke rose to the roof and did not bother us. When

44

it descended lower we left our chairs and sat on the floor, and at last when it eddied round our heads we lay down flat to take one last gaze at the fire before we had to put it out or suffocate.

My establishment of course included a kitchen. As is usual in Africa, because of the smell of cooking and the heat and also because the kitchen is given over to the black servants, it was a separate building a short way from the house on the slope of the hill. The native building, with baked mud walls and palm-leaf thatch, contained a table, a cupboard, and an old iron stove which burned wood.

As a rule one does not waste many words over a kitchen. But I must dwell on it a little longer here, because it is in the kitchen that African and European requirements come into a conflict which for the Negro is almost insoluble. A native palm-leaf thatch is really watertight only when the smoke of a fire on the open floor is forced to find its way out through the roof and closes all gaps by so doing. A kitchen stove, however, is provided with an excellent smoke escape of its own. In order to adjust this discrepancy the sensible compromise was to end the stovepipe just inside the roof instead of taking it through to the outer side, and so the smoke was forced to seek an outlet through the roof. Occasionally, of course, bits fell down from the roof into the pipe, until at last the stove would not draw. Then the cook had to push a stick vigorously down the pipe and clear a channel for the draught. One day a tornado swept through the kitchen and shot a lot of glowing embers straight up the pipe; in a second the whole roof was ablaze. The cloud of smoke and the outcry soon brought me to the scene. The boys were running about like mad with tiny pots and pans of water, which they then tried to throw upwind on-to the blaze. Most of it, naturally, was blown back into their

45

faces and they were soon soaked. But the fire got its first real
hold and began on the windward side when one of them had
the bright idea of pulling the roof down. Now it blazed like a
balloon factory. And as there was no longer any hope of putting it out, salvage was begun. Many onlookers took a hand,
and the salvaging was carried out with a wild outcry and
much running about, while commands flew to and fro. I was
not able to observe what happened to the salvage. All I saw
was the flour being tossed out of the windows, caught by those
outside, who carried it off in their clothing. Soon the kitchen
swam in water and the salvages were plastered all over with
paste. When the roof had burnt out and the fire died down, the
damage was not so very great. Nearly everything except what
had been salvaged was still there. I learnt my lesson, and the
next time the rethatched roof caught fire, as it was bound to,
since it was essential for the pipe to end just under the roof,
all I did was to have the roof removed on the leeward side
instead of on the windward, until the fire went out of its own
accord for lack of nourishment. This time salvaging was abso-
lutely forbidden. The third time, had it occurred, would have
gone even better, but I now insisted on a large piece of corrugated iron being interposed between the end of the pipe and
the roof. So after that we did without these popular entertainments, and the kitchen resumed the humble part it was
cast for.

The appointed master of this highly combustible building
was a young Baszi called Massa. His real name was Tannewujé,
but as this was too long a name the monks had changed it.
Massa was as true as steel. He went with me everywhere, once
even on leave to Germany. He was a splendid fellow, and in
spite of his dignity as headboy he had a great sense of humor.
He could act as interpreter in any number of Negro languages,

and ended by speaking German too; he understood his master and his wishes, was always eager for work day or night, was an excellent hunter, did not steal, lied very seldom, and only occasionally drank more than was good for him. He was always involved in affairs with women, but his morals improved as the years went by, and he had his harem of three wives with four sons. In spite of being the doctor's head servant, he would have no truck with European medicine, and though he had lived so long in the mission, he was true to his own religion. Even when he accompanied me to Germany he took his fetish with him in an old cigarette box. For his part, he refused to recognize the achievements of civilization, and as justification he quoted his father's reply when he asked him once what was the meaning of "civilization." "My son," his father replied, "in our hut the wood fire gives us light at night. It is not very bright, but it costs nothing. You know the new light"—he meant the hurricane lamps—"the white man has brought into our country. They don't cost much either, and they give a brighter light. But do they burn wood? They burn oil, and that you have to buy. It is not dear, but you have to buy it over and over again, and if you cannot procure it the lamp is darker than the fire of our hearths. That is civilization—beware of it!"

There would have been no export trade to Africa had all Negro fathers been as wise as this one and all sons as obedient.

Good fellow and trusty servant as Massa was, he was a wretched cook. Even when later on my wife took charge of the household she could never rely on him. She always had to keep an eye on him and tell him what to do. Yet he was prouder of his poor performance in the kitchen than of all his other very real capabilities. It was particularly bad in the early days, when I lived alone as a bachelor. Massa was so hopeless that he could not decide on the menu without help, even for a single day, and of course we never both thought of it at the appropriate moment. Consequently twice a day he used to turn up somewhere in the hospital. When I saw him hovering about with an embarrassed air I knew at once what he was after, but did my best to ignore him. But the moment I glanced in his direction, a large grin accompanied the unfailing question, "What eat?" As a rule I tried to get rid of him with a curse. Sometimes this succeeded, but not often. Usually he was back a few minutes later at some window or other to remark from a respectful distance, "Not know." As I was not much better endowed with a culinary imagination, I had to solve the problem by laboriously working out the meals for a week, and so they went on until I had some better inspiration. Other remarkable difficulties arose. For example, the Sunday duck. Every Sunday the duck was beautifully roasted except for its hinder part, which was completely charred. I sent for Massa and complained. "It *is* so" was his answer, which of course left me no wiser. "No other way. The duck's tail must so." I did not understand that either. Nor did I care. I merely ordered for the following Sunday a duck with an unburned tail. Sunday came and once more the tail was a cinder. Whereupon my gall rose. I rushed to the kitchen and raised hell. But on the third Sunday, to make sure, I took my stand by the stove to convince myself of the folly of "the tail must so." And now I have to confess that light suddenly dawned upon me. In my kitchen there was, indeed, nothing else for it; we had no oven, and the duck was roasted in a pot. But our largest cooking pot was not large enough to contain the duck. It had to lie at a steep slant with its hinder part sticking out between the pot and the lid. A good hot fire with the flames meeting overhead was required in order to roast the duck, and so, of course, its pro-

48

jecting tail end had to be burnt. "You see yourself, it *must* so." I was beaten, and could only order a larger pot.

But the best of all was when Massa was to serve goulash with fried potatoes. The meal began. Fried potatoes were presented. "And goulash?" "O Lord, have forgotten!"

A Giszi named Tumba acted as houseboy. Tumba was the unobtrusive kind of servant, who says little and keeps himself to himself. He worked well. All I remember of him is his love of my tooth paste, which he was always relishing on the sly.

To these two I looked for my personal comfort while at Bolahun, and they made a thoroughly good job of it as far as lay within their powers. But besides me they had my livestock to look after. As soon as the Negroes discovered my love of animals, I was always being brought all kinds of animals either as presents or to buy. I kept a small zoo the whole time I was in Africa.

Cows, goats, sheep, and hens were, of course, kept for domestic use. The natives of Liberia know nothing of milking cows; and, in any case, their cows have very small udders and give very little milk. Nevertheless, I tried with the help of a man of the Hausa tribe to extract some milk. What little success I had was dearly bought, for their cows are armed with powerful spreading horns, and by the end of it I was black and blue. So my cows and goats were kept only as providers of meat. The hens, again, were not used to a henhouse. They roamed about all day and vanished at night up some tree or other. This way of life meant that they were usually missing, and then being offered to me for sale. I soon gave up poultry keeping, and came instead to an arrangement with Massa that whenever I desired a fowl or an egg it was to be there. This worked perfectly. How Massa pulled it off I never asked. But I certainly never lacked either for a bird or an egg.

Bolahun

My pets gave me more pleasure. Above all, there were my two apes, who played what havoc they liked in my house. Monkeys, amusing as they are, should in my opinion be confined to bachelor establishments. When Massa, for example, came to me with the complaint "Monkeys eat bread again," what it meant was that they had not only eaten bread, but that at the very least the marmalade pot was on the floor, sardines all over my writing table, and the ink upset. And so it came to this at last—that they were allowed indoors only when I was there myself. The same held good for the three small chimpanzees who often consoled my lonely hours with their drolleries.

I shared my home also with many temporary and undesired guests such as cockroaches, lizards, ants, beetles, flies, and gnats. But most unpleasant of all were the snakes, which were to be found all round my house. A particularly inquisitive one invaded the W.C. and my bedroom. All snakes are on principle regarded as poisonous by the natives, and so whenever one was seen it was at once killed with a great hullabaloo and excitement. Nevertheless, there were remarkably few accidents, and patients with snakebite were extremely rare at the hospital. But I had a very unpleasant snake-encounter myself.

Close to my house there was an outcrop of rocks round which the forest had been felled. I was having a summerhouse erected there from which to see the sunset, and the boys at work on it found a regular nest of serpents. They killed sixteen and laid them out in a row at my door for me to see on my return from the hospital. I rewarded them suitably and then went on up the hill to see how the work was progressing. There was a wonderful view in every direction, and to enjoy it I sat down on a large rock which lay apart from the rest and was netted over with rooting tendrils of various kinds of creeper. I had hardly sat down when I felt a sharp pain on the outer side

50

of my thigh. I sprang up and was just in time to see a short brown viper dart away and disappear; I had taken it for one of the trailing roots. The marks where the fangs had struck were clearly to be seen on my white shorts. I ran as fast as I could to the hospital, and after giving myself a local anesthetic I cut out the flesh round the very visible bite. Sure as I was of having done this quickly enough to intercept the poison, it gave me a very peculiar feeling to have to wait to see whether anything would happen. The suspense was soon relieved when the monks, who had heard of my accident, came along with the most trusty of domestic remedies—a bottle of whisky. The internal administration of alcohol as a treatment for snakebite may be out of fashion, medically speaking, but I must confess that after emptying the bottle among us I was not at all sure that, medicine apart, the older doctors were not the better men!

Another time a native brought me a young python. He had hold of it by the back of the head, and it was wound round his arm. He had no fear of it, as these snakes are not poisonous. I wanted to buy it. But when we got on to my veranda and I took a closer look at it I was not at all sure that it was in fact a non-poisonous snake. While he held it I cautiously opened its mouth with my pocketknife and with it I lifted up two fine poison fangs. The boy gave one look, and then with a cry of terror he let go of the false python and took a flying leap over the balustrade of the veranda. I followed him in a flash. We then got hold of a couple of handy sticks and cautiously made our way back to the house. The snake had gone and search as we might was not to be found. But it took me some days to feel quite at home again in my own house.

Such intruders as these into my domestic privacy were always thoroughly upsetting. I must now tell of another less dangerous invasion.

One evening when my work was done I was sitting on my veranda and reading the most recent three-week-old newspapers by the light of the last rays of the sun. Suddenly I saw three large cockroaches scuttling up the wall. Before I had done wondering what made them set out on their travels with such determination I saw ten or twelve more hastening across the veranda. That was not all; the whole place sprang to life. Lizards joined in, and four or five frogs, who as a rule never honored me, came hopping. Hens ran along cackling loudly. It seemed that the smaller creatures had a rendezvous at my place. If I had not been such an African greenhorn I should have known at once what was up. The ants were on the move! Whatever lives and can stir at all flees before them. I suspected nothing, and only tried in the fading light to shoo all these creatures away. Suddenly I felt my legs itching. I was swarming with ants, and now I saw that the whole veranda was alive with them too. At last I understood. The ants were here. Quickly I set fire to the first papers I could lay hands on, to give me standing room at least. Then I shouted for Massa while I hurriedly stripped off my shorts. Ants everywhere! Massa came rushing up. As soon as he saw me in such strange disarray he knew at once what was the matter. But it was too late. He jumped back in horror, tearing off his clothing with wild contortions, itching all the time, ants all over him. I sent him straight off to the hospital for a strong solution of lysol. Meanwhile I kept the bonfire going all round me so as to have a free pitch to stand on. I saw now that the ants approached the veranda from three directions, coming on in three broad columns of hundreds of thousands, while the leaders fanned out and instantly devoured every living thing they could reach.

52

The cockroaches mostly escaped, either by flying away or else by taking refuge on the roof and going into hiding there. But the frogs were lost. Wherever they turned in their terror there was no escape; they were in the thick of the swarm, covered with ants. After a hop or two they sat motionless, and soon they were just balls of black ants. In a few hours nothing was left of them but their skeletons.

At last Massa returned with a bucket of lysol and we set to work together to inundate the ants with it. They died of it instantly, and even the smell seemed to upset them and turn them back. The first thing was to clear a place to stand on, and then I poured a good dollop on the three approach routes, which immediately were strewn with hundreds of dead. They were now thrown into the utmost confusion, some giving ground, others surging on from behind. One more dose of lysol and they saw our game; all turned back. Slowly the whole veranda and then the balustrade were cleared of the enemy, and at last we could breathe. By the light of the lamp—it had meanwhile gotten quite dark—we made a deeper reconnaissance. The ants had not given in! They had struck off from the main route of their attack and were now scaling the wall of the house and then wheeling in order to descend upon the veranda. First, the so-called soldier ants, fine fellows with antennae shaped like the claws of a crab, swarmed out in all directions. Then in closer formation more soldiers followed on, and last the black flood of the regular ants flanked by soldiers who, with their backs turned to the advancing horde, reared up on their hind legs and extended their menacing forceps in the air. The closed ranks of the marching column itself was about two inches wide, and the whole array pressed on in fevered haste. Lysol on the wall! Of that gallant host, scarce one ant escaped alive. It was all of engrossing interest. Lamp in hand I ran

53

hopping round the house, only to learn to my horror that the column I had diverted from the veranda was the extreme left wing of a well-organized attack on my house. The center of the forces involved had pressed forward in the direction of my bathroom, and as there was zinc netting there, the head of the column was already inside the house. On the other side the main attack was parallel with the wall, and only a few groups had penetrated the door and window cracks. On the fourth wall the two flank columns had united, and now they scaled the wall in great haste. To count such multitudes would be impossible. There must have been millions. There was no time to lose then, if I wanted to sleep in my house that night. Massa smeared his legs with lysol and ran round the house soaking all four walls with lysol. This operation meant annihilation, and at the cost of thousands of dead the attack was called off. The whole host was now reformed for retreat, and this is no exaggeration. First, they all fell back in countless companies upon the center, where for a time there was wild commotion until suddenly a new closely packed column emerged out of the confusion on a four-inch front, flanked by angry soldiers in warlike array. Thus the enemy swept on past the house, heading for the forest as though nothing had occurred.

They could still be seen in their unbroken march until eleven next morning. By then the last stragglers had vanished from my house and the whole horrific nightmare was over. My cat was regaled for some days after on terrified cockroaches and a few surviving frogs. But my monkey Fips came off badly. For him the heaps of dead ants were as manna from heaven, only he never noticed that they were soaked in lysol. He died a miserable death the day after, and so I did not escape without loss.

You can, of course, let these ants into your house. They

devour only the living, but without discrimination and to the bone. The natives themselves are as a rule not at all annoyed if they come and rid their houses of rats, snakes, and all other undesirable housemates. But unless you wish to be devoured yourself, you have to clear out of the house. Often they come by night, and before their bites have waked you the whole house is alive with them. Then run for your life! It is too late then for lysol. That will only cut off their retreat. You must wait until they withdraw of their own accord, as they usually do in a day or so.

Animals shut up or tied up near the house often suffer a terrible fate when the ants attack at night. Once at Bolahun I had a young chimpanzee completely devoured, and later my wife lost her great crested eagle. Men overcome by weakness of fatigue on a journey have been known to fall victims. In earlier days, so I was told, men condemned to death were thrown to the ants as a peculiarly horrible method of execution.

To watch their battles with other ants is of great interest. I once saw a whole tribe of termites put to flight by driver ants. White or gray termites are almost defenseless against driver ants. They do not seem to possess the same intelligence or powers of organization. They rush wildly about hither and thither in small companies; the soldiers of the driver ants throw themselves ferociously on the edges of these whirling groups and seizing the termites by ones or twos drag them to the rear, where they are devoured in a trice by their main body. Some again charge like berserkers into the midst of the seething enemy, where they are fallen upon by ten or a dozen termites with whom they fight it out in an indistinguishable *mêlée*. Apparently they have no idea of mutual help. Each fights his own battle whatever the odds.

There is a large variety of red ant, resembling our own wood ant, which is much more warlike than the termite. With them the driver ants sometimes fight pitched battles. One of our monks once had the good luck to see one of these engagements which lasted for several days. The most astonishing part of it was that they broke off the battle at nightfall, but resumed it in the morning.

Can we wonder that the Negroes call the driver ant the mightiest beast of the forest? Even the elephant flees before him! Apart from driver ants, which paid me several visits during my years in Africa, the only other creatures I was acquainted with in such numbers were locusts and flying foxes, which arrived in flocks and droves of million upon million. Fond as I am of animals, I lose sympathy with them in such numbers.

Otherwise the fauna of the African forest was for me the best and most interesting part of my life out there. So I planned to penetrate farther into the great green gloom of the trees. But before I could carry out my plans events in Bolahun came to a head and forced me to defer them for the present.

It was a great day for me when one morning I led a black foreman and six boys into the forest and marked out the site which the new hospital town was to occupy. It was no use telling them; I had to mark it out exactly or they would assuredly have got it wrong. The next thing was to clear the ground. No European forest can give much idea of what that meant. Amid the impenetrable thicket of trees, bushes, and scrub, with lianas slung in all directions, there were dead and moss-covered skeletons of trees, giants of the forest, fallen long ago, which moldered slowly away and made a bed for many new growths of parasitic plants. The way was in places completely barred by the exposed roots of mighty trees, boulders, centuries-old ant heaps taller than a man, and spiked rattan palms grow-

Dr. Werner Junge

Dr. Junge's house at Bolahun

First from left: Doctor Njuma
First from right: the Matchbox

Fafulekolli, the old chief

A chieftain on the road from Voñjama

Newly built hospital huts at Bolahun. This picture was taken on the day before they were opened

Mother with Frambosie case. Note the "ticket" around the child's neck

Palaver house in Bassa

Native village (Buszi)

Fafulekolli's tomb, on the site of his house

ing parallel with the ground. In such places light had to be let in step by step with the bush knife before the trunks of the large trees could be got at with ax or saw. It was hard work in the moist and sultry heat, and these hefty boys took it on for a shilling a day. The required area was cleared in about a fortnight and soon the whole clutter and tangle of felled trees and branches had dried in the blazing sun and were burnt where they lay. The charred trunks were then sawed up and rolled to one side. The removal of the great rocks was heavy work too. The ant heaps were left and later used as baked mud for the building of the houses. Nothing now remained but the great branching roots of the larger trees. As we were unable to dynamite them, they had to be laboriously dug out, and I was utterly astonished at the way the boys went at the digging out and wrenching up of these huge ironhard knotted roots. When that was done the ground was cleared with pick and shovel, the main thoroughfares laid out, and channels for the rainwater dug on each side of them.

I spent all my spare time on the site. But often I had to leave my work to make brief inspections, which was all the more difficult because the number of patients just then was rising daily, and also I was ill myself. For days together I had a slight temperature of which I tried to take no notice. But at last, after a heavy operating day, I had to give in, particularly as my face was covered with a rash of small red spots which soon spread to my whole body. It was obviously chicken pox, but I was puzzled by the constantly rising temperature. Finally, an obstinate boil came out on my neck, and having no medical help, I had to lance it myself at the risk of my life. By this time I had had quite enough of illness and resumed work. But all the same, I was glad when the monks suggested sending for a second doctor, as I was not at all struck with the idea of having, perhaps, to remove my own appendix.

Meanwhile work on the new town had been going with a swing. We now needed over a thousand stout poles for building the houses, and at first we could see no way of procuring them cheaply. Then we hit on the idea of asking each patient for a pole instead of the "iron" usually paid for his ticket. The plan worked splendidly: every morning hundreds of patients arrived at the outpatients' department armed with long poles, and soon we had all we needed.

It was now about the time when the great rains began, and it was noticeably chilly; there was a corresponding increase among the sick of chills and colds and acute pneumonia, a disease the Negroes have surprisingly little power to resist. Complications piled up, and the hospital was crowded with serious cases which called for great care from both doctor and nurses. So I was not particularly surprised when one day the nuns' cook was brought in with a high fever. As I could find no other symptom beyond the fever itself, I thought at first that it would turn to pneumonia. The fever rose to 105 and 106 degrees, the patient became delirious, raved, fell out of bed, and began to roam about with wild and staring eyes; and still, to my shame, I could not make a diagnosis.

At this very time I had among the serious cases in hospital a poor little humpbacked girl named Uata, suffering from a bad inflammation of the marrow of the thighbone. I had always shrunk from this very trying operation, but had finally risked it, and now a few days after the operation she too was in a raging fever. I was grievously worried.

I became even more worried when next day Kamo, the nuns' cook with the obscure fever, suddenly developed a quantity of small spots on his face which next day had spread and become small black pimples. Like so many doctors nowadays, I had never seen a genuine case of smallpox, but there was no doubt this time. With a heavy heart I found the diagnosis of smallpox forced upon me, and it was naturally a heavy blow. None of the natives at Bolahun had been vaccinated, and I had left a smallpox case among the other patients. There was every likelihood that this spark might set the whole of Bolahun in flames; and when I thought of having to fight a regular small-pox epidemic singlehanded in this remote place my heart stood still. Before the danger got out of hand I decided first of all to cancel all operations and to take steps to isolate the case. There was available in the old outpatients' department a bed which I had used for examining patients. Kamo was now moved and put into this bed, but the care and nursing of this one case was no light task, as only Jutta and house surgeon Njuma, besides myself, had been vaccinated and were therefore immune to infection. So we had to take full charge, and we were never done changing and disinfecting and washing. In case of worse to come, I carefully examined all our other patients for symp-toms, and confirmed my fear, for a start, that Uata, the hump-backed girl on whom I had just operated, was suffering from the same mysterious fever.

I had now to reckon on further cases, and so I had an isola-tion hut for about ten beds built with the utmost speed. No fresh patients were taken on, since the infection was within the hospital itself, and no patients released until I knew for certain that they were not infected.

I eagerly awaited the lymph for which I had telegraphed to Freetown; every day now there were fresh cases. One after another my hospital patients had to be moved into the isolation hut.

I was particularly anxious about Momo, the fifteen-year-old

son of an old blind Buszi chief. For years he had suffered very gravely from the yaws. He had lain in his hut for weeks and months covered with large tumors and with his knees contracted. When contrary to all expectations, he at last recovered, his knees were fixed at right angles owing to the contraction caused by his scars, and he was unable to walk; he could only creep on his hands and feet like a spider. After that he sat all day long in the open-sided village palaver house, watching the boys of his own age at play or listening, in his blind father's company, to the talk of the elders of the tribe. He was his father's youngest son and was noted for his intelligence and thoughtfulness; in spite of his extreme youth he was allowed to have his say in the councils of the elders, and soon the whole tribe was resolved that Momo should succeed his father as chief. Then he heard of the white doctor at Bolahun and asked his father to send him there. The chief, who had known the good old days of tribal feuds, slave raids, and human sacrifices, had no opinion of civilization, European medicine, and Christianity, but he could not bear to refuse his favorite son. After a number of troublesome operations I had at last put the young chief on to his feet, even though both his legs were in plaster, and his face beamed with joy when he first walked by himself with the aid of crutches. Is it surprising that he was now my greatest anxiety? So far he was all right. But the first of my nurses to catch smallpox now caught it; he was a young Giszi whom I had taken on two months before owing to the continually increasing pressure of work. The mission school too began to succumb, whereas the hospital town had a clean bill.

If only the lymph would come! To fight the disease merely by disinfection and isolation was to fight a losing battle. Slowly the epidemic gained ground and seemed likely to overwhelm us. The isolation hut was full, and we had to put smallpox cases in the hospital itself. In spite of all this the stream of out-patients never diminished. Again and again we gave them the only advice we could—to go home and come back later. They saw no reason to. "The doctor will soon have the illness in hand," was their reply. And they stayed.

Meanwhile the stage had been reached when the smallpox pustules had broken and were suppurating. Flies descended upon them in hundreds, and the burden on us few who were protected by vaccination was crushing. But by degrees it seemed that our all but hopeless battle to prevent the disease's spreading was, in spite of everything, to meet with success. The daily incidence of fresh cases fell off. Momo, the blind chief's son, was still safe, but Uata, the little humpback, was dying. One night she had a severe haemorrhage from her recent opera-tion. By emergency measures we could easily have saved her from the effects of the loss of blood, but this accident had too gravely weakened her resistance. We had our first death from smallpox.

I did not want any of our unvaccinated staff to enter the infected isolation hut, so house surgeon Njuma and I had to arrange for the burial according to native rites. We wound Uata in her blanket and then in a large piece of matting, and tied this long roll with rope to a stout pole, and so carried her out in her primitive bier. Outside two boys took over our burden and bore it to the burial place, where they laid the pole over the grave and cut the ropes with their knives. As soon as the corpse had fallen, the grave was filled in without ceremony in their heathen way and the soil trodden down with uneasy laughter. Uata was at peace.

Next morning a great tumult arose in the hospital town. A party of excited natives armed with spears came running to my house. "We have to drive our spears into Uata's grave to keep her safe there. Last night she appeared to some of our women and throttled them in their sleep!"

A humpback is always a mysterious being in the eyes of the natives, and the horrible disease of which Uata had died was an added reason for the nightmares several women had had. Of course, they were far too agitated to accept any such explanation and were convinced that the dead girl was visiting them by magic.

The stabbing of Uata with spears was more than I could tolerate. I told the boys to go home and report at once as outpatients if they were afraid. I would give them a magic drink, and the dead would have no power over them. So at the hospital we mixed a bucket of water with a little trypaflavine, a harmless greenish-yellow fluorescent liquid, and gave hundreds of disturbed and excited natives a good gulp of our "funk-medicine." The effect was highly successful. Poor Uata made no further appearance.

Even when more deaths followed, the occupants of the hospital town slept in peace. It seemed now almost certain that the epidemic was on the ebb; but the care of the serious cases only made greater demands—until at last one night the long-awaited messenger arrived with the lymph. The thousand doses he brought were far too few, but I could protect those who were in greatest danger. Jutta and Njuma could be relieved by the nurses, and as long as Momo kept well for a day or two he too would be saved. For the first time for weeks I slept in peace.

With the lymph in my pocket I set off early and in high spirits for the hospital. From far off I waved my precious remedy in the air, hoping to bring a smile to the worn faces of Jutta and Njuma, who were standing listlessly at the door of the isolation hut. It was no good, and my own enthusiasm quickly evaporated when I heard that smallpox had now fastened upon Momo after all. Too late!

It was indeed too late. Five days later Momo was dead. "*Loketa*, when I am well, we will both go to my father and you will give him new eyes." Those were the last words he said to me.

He was our last smallpox case and also the last to die. Suddenly the epidemic faded out. Momo might have been the sacrificial victim who had released Bolahun from the terrible scourge. His death was the price of our release, and later, when smallpox was raging all round us, we remained immune.

It was vaccination which wrought this miraculous deliverance. I divided the thousand doses into two thousand and so was able to vaccinate every one belonging to our little island in the forest. Then followed a tremendous cleaning, disinfecting, and tidying up, and our work quickly began to run on the old lines again. The storm had passed.

All told, we had about sixty cases, including about twenty deaths, among which unfortunately was that of the young Giszi, the only member of the hospital staff to catch the disease. Once smallpox had got a hold on this community of unvaccinated persons it might well have exacted a worse toll than this, and I was decidedly pleased with our successful resistance, conducted, as it had to be, with such meager resources.

When Kamo was released from hospital, pockmarked but cured, his beaming face reminded me that he had been the first or second case and that I had never, in the pressure of work, asked how smallpox had actually reached Bolahun. The incubation period for smallpox is from ten days to a fortnight. Kamo and Uata were the first cases and they both fell ill at the same time, Uata in hospital and Kamo outside. The third case followed eight days later, probably owing to infection by one of the two earlier ones. How had they caught it? About fourteen days before they fell ill both of them—Uata and, as I now recollected, Kamo too—had been in hospital. Kamo had been treated for diarrhea. It might safely be supposed, therefore, that both had been in contact at that time with some carrier of the infection.

Who was ill at that time? The *loketa* himself had had a temperature and chicken pox! Probably it was not chicken pox he had had, but genuine smallpox, though in a mild form because he had been vaccinated three times.

But where had he got it from? The sick register gave the answer. Twelve days before the doctor's illness a child had been treated for what was diagnosed as measles. So this case of measles was smallpox.

This was how the infection had entered the hospital, and this explained too why the hospital town had remained so miraculously immune. And I myself had been a link in the chain which caused the deaths of Uata, Momo, and the rest.

When this was brought home to me my pride and glory in being the conqueror of the epidemic were gravely damped. And also, once the tension of those anxious days was released, I was conscious of a very real exhaustion and enervation. I had sent Jutta off on well-earned leave immediately the epidemic ceased; and now that she was back again, looking well and sunburnt, I began to wonder whether I ought not to have a break too, if I was to keep abreast of all the work ahead of me. The monks insisted that I should have a rest, and so I gladly gave way. I went to the hospital and told "my people" that I was going to "sit down" for two weeks, and bade them have patience till then.

This "sit down" belongs to the Negroes' own scheme of life, and therefore my announcement was received without a murmur. Sitting down, of course, was very far from my intention. Now at last I could fulfill my long cherished wish to penetrate deeper into the forest in search of big game. Besides this, there was my eagerness to seek out the blind chief, Momo's father, in the hope of disarming his rage, consoling his grief, and perhaps, in spite of all, winning his friendship.

CHAPTER 4

Intermezzo

ONCE the decision was made everything happened quickly. As I was after game, I did without the comforts which usually accompany a European on his travels; on the other hand, I wanted to recuperate, and that meant an assortment of what might well be necessaries. Of these the most important was a good stock of provisions, as it was now the "hungry time" just before harvest, and I could not count on much from the inhabitants. And I did not wish to be altogether dependent on my rifle. Rice, flour, fat, tinned meat, and some tins of fruit were therefore regarded by Massa as indispensable, besides his pots and pans. The larger and more unwieldy things went inside the famous zinc bathtub, with the filter, a bottle of whisky, a few bottles of beer, two hurricane lamps, and a reserve of paraffin in bottles. Camp bed, folding stool and table, and some blankets made up another load. Then there was also a tropical tin trunk containing clothes, medicine chest, books, cartridges, and other personal necessaries. Rifles, film and photo apparatus, water bottle, and bush knife were in Massa's personal charge. As porters for the other loads I picked out five strong boys who, in return for free food and threepence a day, volunteered to go with me.

Just before we started one more volunteer turned up—a lean, gray-haired old Negro who had heard that I was out after game. He leant on his old muzzle-loader and said that he had accounted for more than thirty elephants and that he knew the forest well round Kailahun-Lukassu, the royal seat of Momo's father, the blind chief. Years ago he had shot his left hand while loading his gun, and it was completely crippled. Nevertheless I took him on, if only to leave him a happy memory for his remaining years. "Keke," ("Little Father"), as he was called, was not of much help to us, but I am sure he talked to his dying day of how he went big game hunting with the white doctor.

Midday came before I was through with the last hospital duties and was able to set off, and our little caravan had scarcely left Bolahun before we knew that the rainy season had set in. The sluices of the heavens were opened. In a moment we were all drenched. The winding trail, wide enough for only one man, was deeply trodden out, and now became a rushing watercourse with a slippery mud bottom. We struggled on, sliding back at each step. It was a wonder that the boys with their heavy loads kept on their feet at all. The leafy roof held up the downpour here and there and, after storing it as long as it could, emptied it on our heads in waterfalls. The sun went down without our noticing, and suddenly darkness was added to the rain and the forest. We felt our way blindly along the hollow path with our feet, bumped our heads against low branches, or got caught up in some invisible obstruction. The caravan strung out into widely separated groups. Helplessly I toiled on in the tracks of a small boy who had tacked himself on to the porter ahead of me and thought only of not losing touch.

Suddenly we were confronted by a river. In ordinary times it was merely a swamp threaded by a narrow stream; now it was a wide expanse of water. But there must be a bridge somewhere. The leading man felt in the dark for posts supporting a tree trunk bridge.

"Here they are!" Yes, but the trunk was now nearly two feet under water. A false step in the darkness in that swollen bog stream might be awkward, and so tobacco and matches were put inside my sun helmet, which, thanks to its rubber cover, was still watertight; then I took to the water, astride on the bridge.

What a sight to see somebody gliding on some unseen conveyance across a stream, up to his neck in water! But there was no one there to see it.

On we went through the dark forest until we were held up by a larger stream which was usually crossed by a ford. Of course no sign of the ford was visible. But the porters couldn't possibly swim with their loads, and we had to wait until the rest came up. Voices rang up through the darkness, and names were called. At last we were all accounted for. We tried to light a lantern with my matches. No good. The matches were damp, and so was the wick. Massa had, of course, forgotten to bring my electric torch. So the ford must be found in the dark.

Some one or other shouted and we all groped about. Holding hands, we advanced cautiously step by step, one behind the other, into the river where the ford was supposed to be.

To my great astonishment the boys had unerringly hit on the right spot. Though the water came up to the necks of most of us, the first boy soon sang out from the opposite bank, and then the long human chain was drawn in unbroken for fear anyone should be lost.

Scarcely had this obstacle been overcome when the doubt again arose as to whether we were all across, for a number of strangers had joined us. The porters waited to make sure, while I pushed on with my companions. We had a hill to climb, and then through the rain we saw the faint reddish light from some

Negro huts. We went towards the fire, round which a few natives were sitting in an open-sided hut.

"*Isser ho*, old men!"

"*Isser ho, loketa!* So you come through the rain and the darkness."

"I told you I was coming, and here I am."

One of them ran to fetch the only chair of the village, but I preferred to sit on a native stool, cut from the three-branched fork of a tree. Then I warmed myself at the fire, for it had gotten fairly cold. Meanwhile we said *Isser* once more. Another of them proudly displayed the scar of his hernia operation, and then they went on to ask how many I had with me and whether it was true that I was going home; that would rejoice my wives. And this year it was a bad "hungry time."

So we talked on, while I dried my tobacco at the fire. Now and then they laughed when I failed to understand them or at the wild blunders I made in talking their language.

Then the rest of the caravan emerged from the darkness and Massa too. The best house in the village was put at my disposal, a hut in which I could not stand upright. My wet camp bed was unpacked and dried before the fire. I had a meal and warmed myself up with whisky. Then we all sat round the fire again and talked. Were all men white in the white man's country? And had I really only one wife, and what did a white wife cost?

I found it quite impossible to tell them that I had not even one. But now the chief came, bringing the obligatory fowl as a guest offering. He brought only a grain or two of rice to show his good will, rice being now very scarce. As soon as he had gone the rest of the company were politely shown out. I lay down in my bed and the rats took over.

For two days more we journeyed on into the Liberian forest.

69

Native villages became rarer and more primitive. Often the women and children began by running away and crying out in horror at their first sight of a white man. By degrees, however, they gained confidence, and then, losing their shyness completely, insisted on touching the white skin for themselves to make certain the color was genuine.

At last we got to Kailahun, the town of Fafulekolli, the blind father of Momo. Exhausted by the day's march, I was glad to rest in the large, open palaver house, where the posts were carved with strange and savage faces. I reclined in a hammock and waited for the porters, anxious about the reception I should have from this powerful paramount chief. And when the porters arrived I was greeted in the chief's name by a tall slender Negro with fine features and clear brown eyes who came with them. His father, he said, was unfortunately prevented by illness from coming in person, but begged me to visit him in his house as soon as I had settled down and had eaten. Then he went outside and pointed to a very fine and very clean house.

No personal greeting, no present for his guest, the plea of illness—did all this mean that I was unwelcomed? I should know when I paid the appointed evening visit.

It was dark when I sent Massa on to announce me and went to the chief's house. It was a rectangular building, whereas all the rest of the dwellings were round. The door, made of one slab hewn from a big tree trunk, opened, and behind the fire burning brightly on the floor, I saw the chief, leaning on his mighty spear. He was a tall, powerful man, and as he stood there with his sightless eyes directed upon me he seemed to be the incarnation of a primeval age.

"*Atju loketa bendu Bolahun? Isser ho, finjah!*" ("Are you the great doctor from Bolahun? Welcome, brother!")

"*Itjo loketa. Manja bendu, Fafulekolli, finja nu, isser ho!*"

70

("I am the doctor, great Chief Fafulekolli, my brother. Greetings to you!")

I had never yet been greeted so. The word brother in the mouth of this old man was meant as a great honor, and I took it as such. Changing his spear to his other hand, he held out the fingers of his right hand in greeting, and while we snapped our fingers together I was able to look at the great Negro prince at close hand.

He must have been well over sixty. A soft red fez covered his gray head. His face, which was expressive in spite of his sightless eyes, was deeply furrowed. For a Negro's, his nose was strikingly narrow, and it was hooked. His thin, dark lips protruded only slightly beyond his deep brown cheeks. On the left of his chin he wore a finger's length of twisted and nearly white beard. In spite of his proud, erect bearing, I could tell from his quick, short breathing and the pulse beats in the prominent veins of his neck that his days were surely numbered.

He struck the spear into the ground and with the help of two Negroes who sprang to his side sat down on the chief's chair. A seat was brought forward for me too, and my opinion that the great Fafulekolli had not long to live was confirmed when I saw that his feet beneath his loose robe were much swollen. Nevertheless, during the conversation which followed he sat on his chair as upright and as proudly as he had stood before me.

After exchanging the customary politenesses I began to speak of his son Momo. I was astonished when I found that I could tell him nothing new. All my news to the last detail had long since sped through the forest to his ears. He knew what success the operations on his son had had and that he had been able to walk upright. He knew about the smallpox epidemic at Bolahun—in fact, he knew this horrible disease from his own experience: "I too should have died of it, *loketa,* had God willed. But he took only the light from my eyes and left me to live. Momo is dead. *Pawa nu tjo bendu, loketa ma num hennang, pawa kamba piu bendu."* ("Your power is great, doctor, but do not forget that the power of heaven is greater.")

I was completely overawed by such greatness of soul, and in my heart I begged the old chief's pardon for the suspicions I had had because of my unusual reception. He was clearly far beyond the understandable human weakness of blaming the doctor for the death of one who was very near to his heart. The news that Momo had been able to walk seemed to him good enough proof that I was a *loketa bendu.* He knew himself that smallpox was stronger than any medicine. After a short silence he changed the subject and discussed the plans which had brought me into his territory. Without awaiting any request of mine, he "gave" me his forests and all that lived in them.

I should need an experienced hunter who could put me on the track of the elephant. The best he had was Mussa, and Mussa should go with me. Mussa, who crouched on the mat at his side, was the tall ebony-colored young man with the eagle-eyes who had greeted me on his father's behalf on my arrival. With a slight smile, as though to excuse himself for an obvious remark, Fafulekolli observed that hunting elephant in the forest was not without its risks and that the safety of each depended on the courage of all, and Mussa was his son, as Momo was.

The best reply, I thought, to this gentle reminder was to assure him that I would gladly trust my life to his son Mussa.

It seemed high time now to conclude the interview, but with a sign and a word or two he dismissed all present except my interpreter, Massa. We sat, all three of us, by the fire. Addressing Massa in a low voice the chief asked him whether I would allow him to touch my face with his hands. I could not refuse him this. Then Massa called the chief's sons back into the room, and I took my leave, deeply moved by my encounter with this true king of the forest.

Next morning Mussa came to my house to discuss our expedition in every detail. He was particularly interested in my 8-mm. Mauser, which seemed to him too small a bore for elephant.

And now I had to give the medicine man of the tribe ten shillings to pay for a sacrificial offering, from which he could judge the best time for us to set off. Secretly I promised him two shillings extra if his magic got us off not later than the following morning. It was then pointed out that I must also have the people on my side; otherwise the old women would make "bad medicine" and hide the elephants in the depths of the forest. So the people too had ten shillings. I am afraid, however, that this money found its way into the pocket of the medicine man, just as the first had done. Late that evening he made it his pleasure to come to me with the final results; he was able to tell me that he had read from the entrails of a goat that we must leave at latest by sunrise next morning if we wanted to find an elephant. For his sage words I then handed him two shillings, as promised. I turned a deaf ear to his remark that the goat was a very large and costly animal.

So next morning we set off at break of day to seek for game in the vast Kongwa forest, where we should not come upon any more human settlements. Mussa led the way at a quick pace with the light, springy tread of the native. A rifle of really modern pattern was slung horizontally from his naked muscular shoulder, and his left arm rested on the barrel, which pointed to the front. In his right hand he had his bush knife, and a small game bag was tied to the belt which kept up his short black pants. His black body, his weapons, and his scanty clothing were thickly smeared with a mixture of palm oil and animal blood, so that no wild beast should get the scent of human beings. I followed him in khaki shirt and shorts, a khaki sun helmet and tennis shoes, with immediate necessaries in my pockets and a bush knife in my hand. Next to me came one of the strongest porters carrying a watertight tropical trunk, containing clothing, blankets, mosquito net, provisions for eight days, and water for three. A second porter carried my camp bed, blankets for the natives, and rice for us all. Next came Massa with my rifle, water bottle, and cameras. Old Keke, who would not be left behind, brought up the rear with his old ancient muzzle-loader.

Even Mussa had indignantly rebutted my disparaging remarks on Keke's old blunderbuss with its flintlock and powder pan. He himself had gone big game shooting with just such a muzzle-loader until he had sold enough ivory to buy himself a proper rifle.

These muzzle-loaders were loaded with an arrow about twenty inches long, the stout iron tip sticking out of the muzzle. Thus armed, the Negroes noiselessly stalk their elephant until they can shoot at close range. Then they vanish in a flash, leaving the wounded beast to rage, but soon they stalk in and shoot again, until the monster collapses. They do not take aim in the usual way, but fire at arm's length. Their guns have no bead and don't need one for shooting point-blank at a distance of a few yards. To keep their powder dry and in case of rain they have a large leather guard over the powder pan. The natives were so well used to this way of shooting that even Mussa loaded his modern repeater with these arrows, in the belief that they were more effective against elephant than a mere little bullet.

I had seen a good deal of the forest, but the parts we now traversed were denser than any I had known. The vast primeval forest of innumerable giant trees was interspersed with wide swamps in which reeds, bamboos, and prickly palm formed an almost impenetrable jungle, and with expanses of bush and grasses, four to six feet tall, entwined with climbing plants.

The going was easiest in the forest of tall hardwood trees. In the swamps I could hardly bring myself at first to plunge knee-deep into the stinking morass, seething with all kinds of worms and insects. Later I got used to it and was only afraid at each step of leaving my shoe behind in the mud. In the dense bush we followed a hunter's trail cut out to a height of about five feet, and about eighteen inches wide. It was terribly exhausting to press on half doubled up along these tunnels hewn in the undergrowth, where the full force of the blazing sun was felt, but not a breath of air stirred. How thankful I was when we had rivers or streams to cross! How deliciously cool the water felt!

Late in the afternoon we reached an open spot on the edge of a stream, and here Mussa proposed that we should spend the night. While the porters, Massa, and Keke built a small palm leaf shelter in case of the expected evening rain, Mussa and I explored the neighborhood for fresh spoor, but found none. We were surprised by a sudden torrent of rain and hurriedly took cover beneath the shelter, which had just been completed. As we were wet already, we had a quick dip in the stream, ate our meal, and lay down to sleep. Mussa silently took over watch by the fire.

When I awoke it was light. The rain had stopped, but it was unpleasantly cold, and I was reluctant to creep out from my two blankets. Massa had already made coffee, but we could not eat our bread until we had expelled the ants which were feasting on it. My bare legs had got badly scratched the day before, so I put on long trousers and bound my gym shoes and trouser legs with strips of lint from the medicine chest, so as to have no further trouble through swamps. When I had stowed away my pocketknife, pipe, tobacco pouch, and matches in my pocket, and tied the bush knife to my belt, I was ready for my second day of stalking in the bush.

The bush was still wet from the rain of the night, and we were quickly wet to the skin once more. We soon left the hunter's trail and went straight through the forest in search of fresh spoor. Step by step a path had to be cleared with the bush knife. We came on antelope and wild pig spoor, leopard, too, and the great imprints of hippo and also old tracks of elephant. On the edge of a swamp we found the carcass of a magnificent wild boar with fine tusks, which had been pulled down by a leopard a day or two before. Thousands of huge bluebottles had settled on the carcass. It was easy to see that the leopard had been gorging on its prey that very night. We also found clear traces of the struggle close by and the leopard's lair.

Now and again hordes of large red and black colobin monkeys with long white tails kept us company, screaming and leaping wildly through the treetops. Bright blue pheasants flew noiselessly out of the trees, little honey birds flitted between the branches, and occasionally we heard over our heads the loud beat of a great crested eagle's large wings. When that happened the monkeys crouched in silence and terror. We disturbed hundreds of brilliant butterflies, and on dead tree trunks there grew lovely orchids and wonderful flowers never seen before, wafting intoxicating scent. Sunbeams in quivering flight darted obliquely through the leafy roof, casting a gentle sheen like subdued limelight into the green gloom through which we followed Mussa's gleaming black naked body, while he, with short sharp strokes of his bush knife, cleared a path.

A sudden halt! Fresh tracks of a large elephant!

We followed them excitedly as far as a small clearing. There we paused, and both porters put down their loads. Keke sank down to the earth to consult his magic. Pulling half a calabash out of his gamebag, he turned it over on the ground and rubbed some small indefinable black object to and fro on it while he whispered his monotonous chant; then he let go of it, was silent—and began the ceremony all over again. After a few minutes he gave us the result. The spirits of dead elephant hunters had told him this: "Before the sun is at its height you will catch up with your elephant. You won't need to cross the wide water." The river, he meant. "The white man will not be afraid, and the elephant will die by his gun." It soon turned out that the deceased were as big liars as their living representatives, but for the moment I was well pleased with the prophecy.

Mussa smiled knowingly and took me aside: "If, *loketa,* it is your wish that we kill the elephant, then you must be as strong as a black hunter and never grow tired, for elephants travel fast."

"Don't you worry about me, Mussa. Treat me as a native and lead the way. As long as I have enough to drink I'll hold out. Massa, is the water bottle full?"

"Yes, sir, quite full."

Inspired by the fresh trail, I put my trust in Keke and Massa without a thought, and dismissed Mussa's cautious doubts as an exaggeration, a mistake I was bitterly to rue before the day was done.

The porters stayed by their loads, with instructions to build

77

a leaf shelter for us that night. Mussa then gave the word *"Amuli"* ("Let us go"), and with impassive face plunged into the bush. I was quickly on his heels, Massa after me, and lastly Keke. The trail led us into a deep swamp, where overturned palms and knee-deep imprints of the elephant's feet, in which three of ours would have gone, showed us the way. Our quarry had trampled about here, tearing up and treading down whatever stood in his path as though to get rid of his superfluous energy. After casting about for a moment, Mussa led us out of the swamp and into the forest. I saw no more of the trail.

I had always supposed that it would be a simple matter to follow the track of an elephant. But I was greatly mistaken. I now learned that the elephant uses his trunk to remove every vine and branch from his path, letting them fall back behind his mighty hindquarters and drape the way he had gone. Mussa often knelt down to pick up fallen leaves to see how heavily they had been pressed to the ground. Sometimes he lost the trail altogether, and we had to wait while he made a wide circle and picked it up again. *"Amuli."* On we went. Sometimes our path crossed other old trails or wide, well-trodden, ancient elephant tracks. Often I marveled at the way Mussa unhesitatingly picked out the right trail from all the others and followed it with a confidence that quelled all doubts.

Slowly I was dissolving in sweat. The way an elephant has of getting through his native forest is exhausting to the last degree for his two-legged pursuer. Up hill, then back in a circle, halfway down, halfway up again, then into the river wading hither and thither, up the bank again a hundred yards farther back, and then along it—thus we followed our lord and master. Once, after an hour's wearisome stalking, we found we were on our own tracks again.

78

We had now been three hours on the trail. I begged for a rest and when I found that my water bottle was not full, as Massa had said, but half full at the utmost my courage began to fail me. I was aching from the fatigue of continually winding my way along half doubled up; my face and my neck burned like fire from the whipping back of twigs and branches let go by my leader. I looked in consternation at my arms, scratched and torn by prickles and thorns and bathed in gore. I might have gutted three elephants with my bare hands. Exhausted and sunk in my own thought, I pulled at my pipe. What a senseless job, and what a hope, to think of tracking and killing an elephant in the very thick of the bush!

But now came Mussa's pitiless *"Amuli."* I had to drop my miserable reflections, and we got slowly to our feet and followed. "Our" elephant's trail now joined that of another fully grown one accompanied by a young one. The two elders had clearly had a talk together while the young one fooled about. So much I could now decipher for myself. Then both had gone their separate ways.

After a short time we came on rather smaller fresh spoor. I fancied to myself that these were the imprints of a charming young lady elephant and ours those of a proud young gentleman. He had stalked round her several times, broken off a few trees and torn down some branches, and clearly had had some success with the demonstration of his strength and beauty, for she had followed him, deepening his powerful imprints with her "gentle" feet. But instead of passing an hour in dalliance, they had gone relentlessly onward. He, to show off, had of course gone straight up the hill where it was steepest and trampled about in the swamp where it was deepest. The trail was not so easy to lose now.

A party of chimpanzees crossed our path with bloodcurdling

79

screeches. But all that meant nothing to me by this time. I dragged my carcass along as though it weighed a ton, and when I tried to stand upright I had to straighten myself with the help of my two hands. As for the silent tread of the game stalker, it had long since been forgotten. I barged my way blindly along, stopping only when so entangled that I could not move.

The sun had long ago passed its zenith, and three times we had swum the great water. Keke's prophecy had been made nonsense of—and Massa with his water bottle full to the brim! There was only a drop left as an iron ration.

On top of everything else came one more hill! I shall never forget it. I never thought I should make it. Besides, it was all so pointless. We panted so loudly and made such a noise that we might have been heard for miles round, and Keke kept stumbling and falling even more often than I did.

When we had got to the top with positively the last exertion we were capable of we suddenly heard a smashing and cracking just ahead of us, and we knew from the heavy thuds of massive feet that we had come straight on our quarry and disturbed it. The show was on!

Our fatigue vanished. Snatching my rifle from Massa, I plunged through the bush at Mussa's heels. The two elephants could not be more than thirty yards from us. We heard them snort, but could not see them. The undergrowth was too dense.

Down hill again! I staggered, tripped, fell, and could not move. But the elephants were away, and there was no sound to tell us where they had got to.

Massa came and disentangled me; he said they had made up the hill again. Splendid! Even Mussa was of the same opinion. All right then. Up the hill again. We quickly got there and were just wondering what to do next, when suddenly

80

a tremendous trumpeting came up to us from the valley below.

Down we went. I felt no more fatigue now, my empty belly rumbled no longer, my thirst had gone. With catlike stealth we crept through the dense undergrowth.

There again—another long-drawn trumpeting! A cold shudder ran down my spine. The elephant could not be many yards from us and we were feeling our way like blind men. Then we crouched low again and listened breathlessly. Keke noiselessly primed his muzzle-loader.

Crack! That was the end of a tree. And that's just where he must be.

"Amuli!" On all fours we wormed our way forward.

How on earth was I ever to shoot? The thicket was impenetrable to the eye beyond three or four yards.

Suddenly our way was barred by a large flat rock. Mussa crept up on to it catlike, and raised himself for a better view.

Instantly he froze.

The next moment I was by his side, having seemed to grow noiselessly from the earth. Fifteen paces from us a huge gray colossus moved about under the trees. And Massa at my back whispered, "In his ear, in his ear!"

The elephant raised his trunk to tear down a branch, and then at last I could make out his ear and his great tusks. It could be only seconds now before he saw us standing there in the open.

Up with the rifle, safety catch forward, sights in line—why does my heart bang like this, and my hand shake so?

I fired. On the mark, I thought. As for the rules of the game, to follow up at once with a second to make sure, and so on, they were all forgotten. I stood stock-still and thought, He's done for, he's done for!

The next moment the whole forest came to life, smashing,

81

crashing, stampeding on every side, behind me most of all. I was alone. I turned round. There was Mussa on the edge of the rock. I sprang to his side. "What's up, Mussa?"

"Look! There's your elephant!" He pointed excitedly at the beast I had shot.

I turned round, and what a sight I saw! There he stood, a bare ten paces away—his mighty forehead, his two ears widely splayed out, his long trunk curled up over his tusks—menacing and terrible!

Alarm and confusion at the whole herd's stampeding round us vanished in face of this immediate peril. Automatically I brought the rifle up to my shoulder, and aimed just below his eyes at the base of the trunk.

It plainly told on him. The next cartridge was in the breach, but he was already making off to the left with a strange staggering motion.

I had another glimpse of him in a clearing a moment later, in time for one more shot, and then the forest swallowed him up.

Mussa threw me his rifle and was off into the undergrowth. A crashing of trees, a deep groaning, and a low organ note—then utter silence.

Suddenly Mussa stood beside me. "Come!" We plunged into the green sea of leaves together. How I got through the thickets as I followed the blood trail on the leaves I cannot imagine. "There—there, *loketa!*" The great beast had collapsed on his knees. His gore was everywhere. The spasmodic quivering of his trunk showed that his wounds were mortal.

I sprang forward and gave him the *coup de grâce* in his brain. Mussa instantly cut off the finger at the tip of the trunk with his bush knife and threw it into the undergrowth as an offering to the spirits of the forest, so that they would not be envious and hide the elephants in the forest next time. Then he uttered his cry of triumph: "I, Mussa of Kailahun, Fafule-kolli's son, guided the white man who killed you. He shot, but I showed him the way!" The spirit of the giant would hear this as it took flight, and the fear and terror of Mussa would be spread abroad.

Proudly I stuck a green sprig in my hat. Hati, the great lord of the jungle, was dead.

The almost unbearable excitement gave way to a glow of pride. It was a full-grown, powerful bull elephant with two fine thick tusks brown with grubbing in marshy ground. We must have blindly singled him out from the grazing herd, which we had heard but not seen. His tail was missing, and a deep scar showed that it might have been caused by a native arrow. My first bullet had gone too low. That was due to the shaking of my hand. But the second and third had been well placed.

I sat proudly on my defeated enemy's back. It had been a fair fight. Stalking game in the West African forests as the natives do it is as exhausting a way of hunting game as you can find. Now the giant had fallen. But I felt a twinge of regret at having killed this magnificent creature only for the sake of his tusks and for the pleasure of the chase.

Now that I was the possessor of these trophies, I decided never to imitate those famous African explorers who could count up to fifty slain elephants. This should be my only elephant. In the future I would confine myself to photographs and films and play no part in the extermination of this noble animal.

While these thoughts were going through my head I drank my iron ration to the dregs. How heavenly now was my pipe! A glance at the sun showed that it must be four o'clock. We had been ten hours on the trail. It would be dark in another two hours, and it was a question whether we could reach our porters and their encampment within that time. Mussa was urgent to be off. Back up the hill—for the third time! Once on the top a council of war was held. We could now either retrace our steps or try to make a beeline for our bivouac. I thought of the ten hours, and hearing only the "beeline" without thinking of the "try" decided on the second alternative.

"*Amuli!*" On we went again through fresh jungle and swamps. At least we had no more need to think of rules of stalking, but to make up for this I was tortured by thirst. I did not dare drink from any of the streams or marshy rills for fear of infection, and I suffered torments.

It began to get dark, and punctually the rain set in. We lost no time in choosing a suitable spot and building ourselves a palm-leaf shelter for the night. I even had a sort of bed constructed for me out of branches and bamboo stems. It was not long enough and fearfully hard, but anyway it saved me from having to lie on the damp ground.

I lined my helmet with leaves and put it out to catch the rain. I also twisted cornets out of large leaves and stuck them upright in the ground, so as to collect a little more water to relieve my burning thirst. Meanwhile Massa had skinned a piece of the elephant's trunk, which Mussa had brought along, and was holding slices of it on spits of green wood over the fire he had lighted under our shelter. Elephant trunk is accounted a delicacy, but to my taste, in spite of my hunger, the half burnt and half raw flesh was terrible. I managed to swallow some of it, drank the rain I had collected, and then I had only one desire—to get to sleep as soon as possible and forget the wet, the cold, and my only partially allayed hunger and thirst.

My wet clothing bothered me, so I took it off. But then I

froze, and, besides this, the primitive roof dripped on me all the time as I lay with aching bones on my hard grill of branches.

So I made up the fire, dried my clothes and put them on again, and sat staring at the glowing embers. My three trusty companions lay huddled together by the fire and slept like the dead. The rain pattered monotonously on the roof and fell in heavy drops with wearisome regularity on me and on the sleepers and the fire, where they petered out in a brief sizzle. The dense smoke of the green wood made my eyes smart and eddied in thick swathes beneath the roof before making its escape into the open.

Hour followed hour. I sat carving little elephants out of the firewood, dreaming and listening to the night sounds of the forest. I could distinctly hear wild boar grunting close by. Monkeys, awakened suddenly by some threat of danger, shrieked in excited chorus and then calmed down. A troop of chimpanzees uttered their piercing yells and took a long time to calm down. Then again, when all was still, I could hear a faint rustling sound. Perhaps it was a leopard prowling round our bivouac or a python enticed and yet alarmed by our fire. In the distance too I heard elephants again. Somewhere—it sounded as though from a hilltop—they trumpeted loudly and fearsomely through the rain and the night for minutes on end. I imagined to myself that they had found their dead companion and that this was their lament for the dead. It was a thrilling and awe-inspiring nocturn.

The twelve-hour tropical night passed with leaden feet, but at last it grew lighter, the rain stopped, and the sun began to illumine the smoking swathes of mist which rose like ghosts from the earth and the glistening foliage.

I awakened my companions from their trancelike sleep.

85

My last painfully hoarded pipeful of tobacco had to do instead of coffee; we stretched our stiffened limbs, and once more set off through the dense bush. For six hours we wearily made our way on, in utter exhaustion, worn down by hunger and thirst, dumbly exerting what strength was left in us. How hard it was now to spare a thought for old Keke, who was at his last gasp. After each breather it was harder to get up again; with every hour the heat was less endurable; with every step the pace got slower.

I now learned at first hand that the secret of energy is the putting forth of one more effort when you know that you cannot go another step.

When, to my sheer astonishment, we reached our first bivouac at midday I did not know which to marvel at more—the unerring instinct which had led Mussa through the trackless wilderness to the right spot or the unquestioning alacrity with which as soon as we had arrived he set off again to fetch the other boys from our first bivouac, two hours distance away.

We others sat or lay in the glowing heat until Mussa came back with the porters and their loads. And now for a long, long drink of water—was there ever such a moment? Then I opened a tin of bully, but I could not swallow the smallest morsel. My mouth and lips were swollen, and now they suddenly began to bleed. I had to content myself with the tins of fruit I had with me. Then we had plenty of strong coffee, I lit my pipe, and all was well again. It was surprising how quickly my deadly fatigue passed off.

We were soon on our feet again and late that same evening we reached the village, where the people streamed from every hut to greet us with shouts of wild enthusiasm.

It was just as well for me that it was dark, because the first glance in a looking glass showed me a horrible sight. Two cadaverous eyes stared back at me from hollow sockets. My sunken face and neck were unshaven, scratched, and caked with blood. All over my body ticks had clung and sucked their fill. My clothing was torn and filthy, my arms lacerated, my gym shoes shapeless lumps of clotted black mud. It was a terrifying sight, and suggested anything but happy hunting. All the same, I was proud and pleased, and after a copious hot bath and a whisky nothing remained but the happy memory.

The whole village was ringing with music and dancing, and although the hour was late, I went, accompanied by Massa, to pay a visit to my "brother," the old blind Fafulekolli. I found him sitting up in his low bed by the fire and struggling for breath. The medicine man and two women were crouching beside him, and at the foot of his couch was Mussa. His freshly oiled black body showed no trace of our hunting expedition, and he appeared to have just concluded his account of it.

I sat down in silence behind my fellow hunter and waited until the old man had got over has attack of breathlessness. I had not been able to examine him yet, but what I saw left little doubt that his circulation was in a bad way.

After a while he raised himself up. "Is the *loketa* here?"

"Yes, Fafulekolli, I have got back. I thank you for sending your strong son with me. With his help we soon killed an elephant. I thank you."

A faint smile came to his tortured lips. "It is good."

I next tried, without being obtrusive, to offer him my help as a doctor.

He started up as though galvanized: "I am not sick. It is not the help of a doctor I need. It is my old enemy, Lormakolli of Laima, who is trying to kill me with his magic, because he

87

wishes to be chief in my stead. But I do not fear his medicine. My magic is the stronger. I shall live."

I ventured on one more attempt and quoted his own words, which he had previously addressed to me. "Your power is great, but that of heaven is greater."

"Kamba szaa!" ("God knows it!")

Slowly he lay back and closed his blind eyes. I saw that my wish to be of help was not to be granted, and silently I took my leave.

Next day half the village, led by the indefatigable Mussa, set off to bring in the meat. I would gladly have joined the expedition in order to witness the dismembering of the elephant, but I was not yet in a fit state to face the rigors of the long trek through forest and bush. Instead I spent the time shooting monkeys and guinea fowl. Besides these and a few tortoises, we bagged, after an exciting chase, a six-foot waran, a black and yellow giant lizard which Massa, who led the field, killed with his bush knife.

Fafulekolli seemed to have got over his collapse of the day before. He was better.

When the villagers returned they brought me a pair of fine large, and unusually straight tusks, which I proudly sent on to Bolahun. In addition, Mussa with a smile gave me the two ears in playful allusion to my first poor shot.

The whole village was now given over to lively scenes of cooking and roasting, although the elephant meat, which was brought in in huge quantities, was, after the lapse of five days, in an advanced state of decomposition and humming with flies. From every hut came the unpleasing smell of high meat, which, however, was far from unpleasing to the inhabitants, who expressed their joy at this welcome addition to the menu in dancing, music, and song throughout the night. It all gave me an irresistible urge to get out of this very noisy and very smelly place as soon as ever I could.

So I bade farewell to Mussa and the proud old Fafulekolli, giving them presents in token of my gratitude for their hospitality. Fafulekolli gave me a costly tapestry which from its weave must have come from the Gold Coast.

I turned round once more as I was leaving. The old chief stood leaning on his long spear in front of his house with his eyes fixed on the sun. This sight of him made an unforgettable impression, because I was so sure I should never see him alive again.

After two days' travel I reached Vahun, where the chief was Ngombu Taetje, father of my orderly Joseph Ngombu (Empty Matchbox). My plan was to return from here to Bolahun after a brief excursion to Pendembu, where civilization and iced drinks were waiting.

But it turned out otherwise. After dark on the day before I was to leave Vahun a messenger from Fafulekolli arrived, begging me to return at once and give him my help as a doctor. I could not refuse my "brother," although I had little desire to plunge into the depths of the forest again. Leaving my porters to follow, I reached Kailahun by forced marches by noon of the second day.

The little town, usually so lively, was silent and dead. I thought at first that I should not find the chief still alive. But when I entered his house he lay as before on his bed by the fire, propped up and surrounded by his sons. He was unconscious. It was obvious that it was thrombosis and that he was beyond help. After being bled he recovered consciousness for a few moments. He asked whether I was there and spoke in a low voice to Mussa, who was supporting him. His dignity was impressive. Not a word of sorrow or complaint.

He was a true King and he died like a king as evening descended upon the village.

His eyes had scarely closed for ever before all the people poured out into the open and raised a heart-rending clamor of lament. His many wives ran about the village in parties of ten or twelve, rending their clothes and tearing their hair and working themselves up into such a frenzy by their unceasing cries that they seemed to be possessed. Other women, and children too, were caught up and carried along by these raving women, who ran hither and thither like terrible incarnations of woe. Hysteria by mass suggestion seemed to be the fate of the whole village. Sleep was not to be thought of. Even when there was a lull it was not for long; the howls of lamentation soon broke out afresh. Towards morning the clamor began to die down, and at last I and the exhausted populace had some rest.

At about noon of the following day I was invited to the palaver house, in the center of the village, in order to attend Fafulekolli's funeral. I found almost the whole village assembled there. Some of the men were inside the building, standing or squatting or sitting on the low balustrade, and some stood about with the women outside. In the middle of the palaver house many robes, cloths, blankets, a few headdresses, sandals, swords, spears, fetishes, earthenware pots and colored leather pouches were heaped on the ground. Massa informed me that all these were Fafulekolli's personal possessions, which were to be buried with him in his grave. Now and then someone stepped forward and laid some "irons," a kola nut, or some other trifle on the heap as a farewell present. Women too with bent heads pushed modestly through the circle of men to add their handfuls of rice to the piled-up wealth. Not knowing what might be expected of me, I inquired

90

of Massa in a whisper, and then contributed my pocketknife, having nothing else suitable on me.

Then the dead chief, lying on a mat, was carried from his home by several men. The body was washed and anointed with palm oil. The mat was laid down in the palaver house, and the chief was clothed in all his assembled robes. One was put on over the other until at last he became a rather shapeless bundle. Then his weapons were given him, with the exception of an iron spear for throwing, bound with colored leather, and a magnificent broad sword in a black leather scabbard, with a hilt of chased silver inlaid with ivory. Mussa took possession of these two weapons. All the rest of his possessions were piled up at his feet, and the four Negroes wrapped the whole up in the mat, bound it to a long pole, and so bore the dead chief to his grave.

The people followed with Mussa at their head. The grave had been dug at the foot of one of the side-walls of his house and was not a very deep one. Three Negroes stood in it up to the waist, and it was Mussa's part to throw them six bundles of "irons" as payment for their labor as gravediggers. Otherwise they would refuse to vacate the grave.

Meanwhile the bearers had freed the corpse of Fafulekolli from the pole, and it was consigned without further ceremony to the grave, which was then filled in. At that moment four or five men stepped forward and fired off their old-fashioned guns into the air. The large crowd of women and children instantly set up renewed howls of lamentation, and the shouting went on without a pause.

The piercing cries and deafening noise quickly drove me indoors, and while we were busy packing up Massa told me that Fafulekolli's house would not be leveled to the ground. The spot where it had stood, which marked also the spot where the blind old chief was buried, would be paved with large flat stones and enclosed, so as to mark for all time the last resting place of this great chief. I had already seen such enclosures in many other villages.

When an ordinary Negro dies the funeral feast is held on the evening of the burial, and the whole village, with the aid of much rum, palm wine, music, and dancing, helps the bereaved to forget their pain and grief. But on the death of so mighty a chief months of lamentations go by before the time of mourning ends in festivities which often last for a week.

To escape the noise of lamentation, which would presumably be kept up all night, I sent a message to Mussa to say that I must be off that same day. After a few minutes he arrived in person, accompanied by the medicine man and some of the elders of the village.

All through these stirring events Mussa had remained outwardly unmoved, erect, and calm; and when I saw him standing there, so earnest and so dignified, it was as though old Fafulekolli was before me in Mussa's form. If he were to be chosen as chief the fate of the tribe would be in good hands.

When I stepped up to him to say good-by he held out his father's sword with the silver hilt. "Fafulekolli on his last day bade me give you his old sword so that you would always remember this: *Your power is great, but the power of heaven is greater.*"

"*Kamba szaa*" ("God knows it") is what I ought to have answered, but I was so deeply moved that I could not speak. Did Mussa know what a message he had brought me with that gift?

I now understood the old man both in his first rejection of the medical help I offered and in his utterly unexpected change of mind as soon as he knew that his end was near. He had

92

carefully noted my last attempts to save him, knowing full well how hopeless they were, and when he saw that they were indeed unavailing and that the parting had come, he had thought, and as he thought of it he had smiled, of this wonderfully touching reproof of the white medicine man's self-assurance.

Indeed I have taken it to heart, Fafulekolli, and all the years I was in Africa your sword hung on the wall opposite my writing table. I had to leave it behind there, but I have never forgotten it nor what you meant by it.

It was a Sunday when I got back to Bolahun, where I found a great deal of work waiting for me. My correspondence had also piled up, and among the other letters I found one from the Liberian Minister of Health, in Monrovia. It requested me to set off at once for certain remote districts of Liberia in order to fight the smallpox which was raging in Sierra Leone, French Guinea and in those parts of the Liberian hinterland lying between the two. The Bolahun district had remained immune. The Government had already made all preparations. Vaccine and a refrigerator for storing it in were on the way. District commissioners and paramount chiefs had been instructed to put themselves at my disposal and carry out all sanitary measures I required. Urgent as the work of the hospital was, I had really no choice but to do as the Government asked.

CHAPTER 5

Doctor and Medicine Man

THE BEST thing that came of the task laid on me by the Liberian Government was the refrigerator. It was suited to our primitive conditions as it was run on paraffin, but it produced real ice, which made the natives dance with delight, shouting "Hot, hot!" when we gave them a piece to hold. Above all, we could keep food, particularly meat, longer and enjoy cold drinks, for which so far we had had to rely on such simple devices as wrapping bottles in wet cloths and hanging them in the wind.

My first task on return was to see at least to the worst cases which had accumulated during my absence. It was one more proof of how necessary it was to have a second doctor at Bolahun to prevent this undesirable waiting list of patients.

For this reason I would not even now have taken on the anti-smallpox campaign had not the district commissioner sent a messenger from the capital of Busziland, adding his plea for the greatest speed, as the whole district was in the grip of the disease.

Nevertheless it was imperative first of all to see the progress of our building scheme, and to give urgent and indispensable instructions without loss of time. On the hill which dominated the town to the north the residence of the new chief was already built, and from there a straight road led to the square market place, already bordered by several completed houses. Even the uncompleted palaver house was easily recognizable.

94

As all except the public buildings were in the same style and of the same measurements, the work went forward almost without a hitch. It was now only necessary to fix the actual position of each house so that they would be built in rows and not higgledy-piggledy. The ant hills had all been made use of as baked mud for the walls, and we now employed women and children to bring soil along from more distant ant heaps or other sources, to mix it, and also to give the walls a final polish by smoothing them with their hands. We were now employing up to seventy boys as a rule, and as the town grew so the iron pieces in my treasury waxed and my store of rice waned. The approaching collapse of my inspired financial policy was clearly to be seen, and now was just the time when the "doctor-money" was due to make its greatest inroads on the rice store. But I saw no reason to dismiss men on that account. If finance ministers of great countries permit themselves to juggle with the taxpayers' money, surely I could indulge in a little inflation of my own.

After this the preparations for my journey went quickly forward. The Government was financing the business, so I allowed myself rather more comfort this time. I took with me two orderlies, one of whom was my house surgeon, Njuma, and we were a party of twenty-six altogether when we finally set off on a day of steady rain. I had to sit in a litter for most of the journey, as I was weakened by continual diarrhea and could not keep up with the quick pace set by the boys.

I was traveling in the opposite direction to that of my hunting trip, and after crossing the mighty Bakufossa mountain we arrived at Kolahun, the seat of a Liberian district commissioner. The great man, however, was at Vonjama, capital of Busziland, the seat of the neighboring district commissioner. So I hurried after him with all possible speed.

Vonjama, a large town of nearly a thousand houses situated on a low flat hill, resembled an army headquarters. All the officials and chiefs of two districts had assembled under the presidency of the Minister of the Interior, who had since left. Musicians, dancers, and all kinds of traveling folk had come into the town. There was even an excited black press photographer from Sierra Leone who aroused mirth and terror with his antediluvian apparatus. Native women in piercingly bright print dresses sat beside the wares they offered for sale; exhausted porters reposed their muscular limbs on the sandy ground; slaves squatted shyly near by in twos and threes. In the shade of a large kapok tree a Negro in a fantastic getup played the snake charmer with live poisonous snakes before a crowd of gaping onlookers. The sick and the crippled squatted by the roadside, begging for alms. Mohammedan priests strode gravely through the throng, and soldiers, bursting with zeal and conscious pride, marched along to the council house, where for the last fortnight discussions had been going on about a general composition of the quarrels of the chiefs, the abolition of slavery as enjoined by the League of Nations and ordered by the President, and also about the smallpox menace.

The contentions between the chiefs had been settled in a very Solomonic manner by cutting up the large chieftanships into several smaller ones. This had the effect of increasing the number of chiefs, but also of diminishing the number of discontented aspirants, even though the great ones grumbled. Upcountry the power of the Liberian Government was none too strong, and it was easier to deal with many small rulers than a few powerful ones. The question of slavery, however, was almost bogged, and not—as might be supposed—because of any protest from the large slaveowners, whose capital was evaporating and whose large coffee plantations, owing to the low price of coffee, were too unremunerative to cultivate, but because of the veto of the beneficiaries of this undesired freedom.

Slave-owning in Liberia had always been conducted in a humane manner. The slave had his house and could marry; he had land of his own to cultivate and payment in the form of presents. All he lacked was freedom, and his one hardship was belonging to the lowest social class. But these two drawbacks combined did not, in the eyes of most former slaves, weigh as heavily as the loss of the social and legal protection hitherto given them by their masters. The new responsibility of having to fend for themselves crushed them to the earth. And there was no help for it now that it had been ordained from on high. Nevertheless, a compromise had been found and forced through the Assembly, but it did not give them any immediate relief. They had been granted the right to remain with their masters, who were released from all responsibility for them beyond paying them a regular wage. And so, after all, they had to make the best of it. Most of them have grown accustomed to their freedom by degrees, but even years later one came across Negroes who betrayed their original status by a craving for subordination.

As I and my small train of porters were making our way through the crowd to the council house the important gentlemen there assembled immediately adjourned and came out to welcome me in the cordial way typical of Liberia. In particular, "my" district commissioner for Bolahun, in whose district my hospital was situated, could not do enough to make clear to all present that I was "his" doctor. He clapped me on the shoulders with both hands and promised me one present after another.

The problem of finding shelter for me and my people was

97

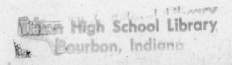

a very difficult one. At last three rooms in a neighboring building were made available, and I moved in.

Before I turned in, an incident occurred which might well have turned out very badly for me. "My" district commissioner, Ware, invited me to supper, and I gladly accepted, not only out of politeness, but in hopes of fresh meat. But when I and the three Government officials sat down to a stew, the meat of which had been hung for at least a fortnight, I knew that a single mouthful would make me vomit, distinguished company or no. It would, of course, have wounded my host to the quick if I had rejected the food he offered me, and for a moment I was completely at a loss how to get out of the predicament. In the nick of time I saw Mr. Ware shaking pepper copiously on the already highly seasoned dish, and at once I uttered a cry of horror and made a face to suit. I said that the dish was far too hot for my European tongue as it was. They burst out laughing at my tender tongue, smacked their thighs, and to show me what a Negro could stand showered the pepper more copiously than ever. After a while their laughter turned to regret, and they very kindly allowed me to have something cooked by my own cook. This saved the situation, and though I had to put up with being laughed at all day long for my tender palate, I could at least dine to my satisfaction.

I took part in the morning session next day and was told that the smallpox had obviously come from over the nearby French border, and spread from there through the whole district. By order of the district commissioner and the chiefs the victims had been immediately isolated; they had to leave the town and take to the forest with all their families and dependents. Nothing more was then heard of them until they either died or returned safe and sound. This elementary form of quarantine was, of course, effective enough, but it had its loop-holes, since nothing was done to prevent the spread of the disease through all the numerous "contacts." It came out later that the number of cases was often four or five times greater than the chiefs were aware of.

After I had made a rough survey of the situation, vaccination began, first of the officials and then of the chiefs and their followers, and this excited universal and respectful astonishment.

The district commissioner had allotted the afternoon to a grand discussion of hygienic matters in general, which owing to the disastrous course it took I have never forgotten. The discussion began by his taking the floor himself and setting forth without the least disguise his own meritorious achievements in the service of the district and its inhabitants. He went on to thank me for having come, hoped we should work well together for the benefit of humanity, and ended with a cheer for the Republic of Liberia. Then the supreme chief of all the Buszis rose with great pomp and delivered an eloquent speech of small substance, the climax of which was that on behalf of the chiefs he was presenting me with a spotless white cock and ninety-nine eggs as a token of their gratitude.

I have always been surprised at the talent the natives have for impromptu speaking. Using every resource of popular oratory and ingenious argument, and often accompanied by a running commentary of approval or disapproval from their always attentive audience, they express their point of view with considerable force and often with unassailable logic. They speak from their places, and as long as the speaker has hold of a rod suspended horizontally from the ceiling he has the ear of the house and cannot be interrupted. As the natives have no script, all speeches are extempore, and for this reason good speakers often enjoy greater fame than good soldiers, hunters, or sorcerers.

So when my turn came to stand up before this select company I had to put my best foot forward. I tried to explain our conception of sickness and what we meant by hygiene; and I spoke of urban sanitary problems, such as the supply of drinking water and sewage disposal, and went on to the endemic diseases due to worms, leprosy, smallpox, and also gonorrhea.

The applause which followed my discourse was more for its manner than its matter, judging from one of the chiefs who rose after me and grasped the rod. He said that my remarks were no doubt very reasonable, but that it would make far too much work to carry out my suggestions. And as for what I had said about the cure and prevention of sexual diseases, it would mean far too great an intrusion upon the private life of the individual. And where was the necessity for it? I had only to look round me to see that they had all attained to a ripe old age notwithstanding.

I was not going to put up with this riposte, so I grasped the speaking-rod and asked him straight out how long he had been a sufferer himself. Four years, he replied. I answered that if he took the steps I prescribed he would not need to suffer any longer. That, he replied, could hardly be so, and once he had got it what was the use of all this hygiene?

The applause which greeted these words showed that he had the majority of his worthy fellow members with him. But the district commissioner thought it right to come to the help of "his" doctor now that he was in a tight corner. Trembling with anger, he reminded them hotly of the duty of the State to care for the health of its citizens, and the interest it had in doing so. Chief Boima at once made the terse rejoinder that he did not see what it mattered to the Government of Liberia whether he had gonorrhea or not. There were other things it might consider with more advantage, such as a reduction of the poll tax. The debate petered out after this, and I left the building with the district commissioner, who was snorting with rage. For my part, I had been greatly amused by this experience of tropical democracy.

It says a lot for the sense of fair play of the natives that the two chiefs who had contradicted me most sharply came up to me after the sitting and assured me, to the accompaniment of finger snapping, that I was a good speaker and a clever man. I understood what they meant and, of course, was not offended by their opposition.

I had, however, come to the conclusion that I should never be able to overcome it by further discussions. More good would be done by trying to convince the important people one by one. I should also have to get down to practical work if I was to fight the epidemic. Every day I spent here was lost time.

So next morning I vaccinated the whole population of Vonjama, and on the day after set off on my journey through the smallpox area. My porters, unfortunately, were not my own carefully selected boys, but some who had been put at my disposal by orders of the district commissioner. At the very outset they were far from enthusiastic over their undesired task, and hence on this journey I had for the first and only time to cope with one of those dreaded so-called "porter palavers." After declaring suddenly that their loads were too heavy, they put them down and could not be induced to go another step.

When anything like this occurs out in the forest the situation is so difficult that you are practically forced to give in. But on this occasion my porters chose an unlucky moment to go on strike. We had just come upon a company of colobin monkeys, and their long silken black fur attracted me. So I left my porters to sit on their loads and followed the troop of monkeys. I had the luck to bag six of these large creatures with formidable teeth. When I hauled my booty along the strikers instantly forgot their grievances at the sight of so much fresh meat. Of course, I was cut to the heart at having to burn it all on the spot, as I could not think of asking them to add to their already excessive loads! Without a word they loaded their boxes on their heads with the monkeys on top, and went their way shouting and singing like children.

Native porters have indeed a philosophy of their own; a Till Eulenspiegel lies hidden in each one of them. If their way goes uphill they break into a run with shouts and whoops, so as to forget their exertions. If a long stage begins to be tiring they sing and joke and pretend to be as fresh as when they started. One of them sings out in falsetto, "Are you merry and bright?" The answer is given in one short, shrill cry by all the panting men in chorus. Then the protagonist asks, "What does your heart say?" To which the answer of the chorus is a deep, drawn-out *"W-u-u-u!"* This brief amoeban song, if it may be so described, is repeated over and over again, and does actually whip up their jaded energy, although both text and music, coming from lurching, sweating, and puffing boys, sounds like the bitterest irony. The physical achievement of carrying a fifty-pound load hour after hour for perhaps twenty miles a day through the forest is something to marvel at, but not more so than the art of carrying such loads on their heads through all the many obstacles to be met with on these treks. Up and down slippery slopes, wading through swamps and streams, crossing rushing torrents at a dizzy height on flattened tree trunks, clambering over great trees which have fallen across the trail or under their low hanging branches when still erect—wherever the path leads the porter follows without ever being known to let his load fall. The native boy's power of endurance and his prodigal expense of energy make him the true but too little recognized hero of all African expeditions.

One of the places we visited with our "anti-smallpox battery" was particularly tragic. Here smallpox had spread beyond the village itself to what is called the Gri-gri Bush. This cult of the West African Negroes, with its mystical and symbolical ritual, is kept inviolably secret; and yet so terrible was the scourge, and so great the terror for their sick children which it aroused, that the people were forced to break the ban laid upon all uninitiated persons and to admit even a foreigner, a white man, into one of their greatest mysteries. It was some help in overcoming their extreme reluctance that I too was a medicine man. Thus it happened that I was one of the very few Europeans to penetrate the mystery of their secret Gri-gri Bush.

The time has no doubt come when this primeval institution must fall a victim to the advance of civilization; and among the civilized Negroes of the coastal region it has already either died out or degenerated into a farce. For this reason I was particularly glad to be able to study it, and among the Buszis especially, who more than any other tribe of the whole Liberian hinterland have kept their racial heritage unimpaired.

The essence and meaning of Gri-gri Bush lie in the bringing up of the boy to be a man, in the indoctrination of the many scattered native settlements with the feeling for racial, tribal, and religious communion, and in the initiation and introduction of the young into the cultural, ritual, and mystical customs of the tribe, so that they are fitted to be in the fullest sense members of it. Respect and reverence for age, for tradition, for law and justice, for the power of the chief and particularly of the medicine man, bodily toughness, and reticence are instilled into the boy as he grows up. All this is clothed in a lavish symbolism and mysticism, which give the secret mysteries of the Gri-gri Bush an influence never outlived by any who have once been initiated.

If the chief and elders of a place want a Gri-gri Bush to be held, the most eminent medicine men of the tribe hold a council and depute one of their number to be Bush-master. This Bush-master now comes under the chief's authority and is responsible to him for all that occurs. He looks for a suitable spot in the forest at about an hour and a half's distance from the village and tells the people its approximate position. The whole bush in this direction is now taboo, and no one who has not himself been through a Gri-gri Bush, and especially no woman, must set foot within it. Anyone who disobeys must die; he is secretly poisoned. Near the village on one of the larger thoroughfares the entrance to the "devil's bush" is plainly marked by a palisade of palm leaves, of palm stems frayed out into besoms; and of bamboos and shredded reeds. In the middle of this palisade there is a small gateway behind a curtain of shredded bamboo. If an unauthorized person passes this gateway he is confronted with a number of tracks, all well trodden and all leading in different directions. Every now and then each track splits up into several branches, each of which dies out, and the intruder, unless he knows his way, is continually led astray. On these paths spells and enchantments are buried to make the undesired visitor blind or sick, and no native would ever dare defy them. At one spot known only to himself the Bush-master buries a charm and plants a kapok tree. This gives the place its sanctity. The Bush cannot break up until the medicine man has taken the charm out of the ground, and not until then can the young men be released. Only he can loose the spell; and if he is prevented, as happened in one case I know of, when the Liberians put a Bush-master in prison, the young men have to wait until he comes back. The kapok tree, however, which may live for a hundred years, maintains the sanctity of the place for all time. Even long after the spell laid on the place has been lifted, the uninitiated will avoid it as long as the single kapok tree stands in the forest.

When a Bush is to be opened a number of devil dancers come into the village on the prescribed day to the sound of drums, making wild and stirring music. One of the dancers wears an enormous black mask of wood with a great crocodile snout; he is the Bush-devil. After a brief, wild dance he sinks down in the midst of his fellow devils. The chief greets him in a long speech, and after it the parents of the boys, who are all seated rather shyly on the ground, throw offerings, usually of money, to the Bush-devil, while they perform a dance of expressive humility, hoping thus to make him well-disposed towards their children. For outsiders the devil is the master in Gri-gri; but the real master is among the crowd, unseen and unknown. Then the devil's spokesman announces that the devil is going to swallow up all the boys and will never give them back in the form in which they now are. Even if he does spit them out again, they will be other people with other names, and no one must call them by their old names.

And now the chief takes the lead by offering one of his own sons to the devil, and the other parents follow suit; all the boys feel more or less frightened. The devil touches each one with his gigantic maw, thus symbolically swallowing him. This bite is held to be the origin of the tattoo scars which the boys later acquire in the Bush. When all his victims have been swallowed, the devil vanishes with his following and also with the boys, who are trembling with fear and have only a dim idea of what awaits them in the forest.

The village keeps silence about the Gri-gri Bush and the children pass for dead; but meanwhile the children themselves, boys of from ten to fourteen, build huts for themselves under the direction of their master, as well as a palaver house and a house both for him and the devil. Until they can harvest the crops, which they must plant and cultivate for themselves, their food is brought from the village by initiates. The unpleasant business of tattooing soon follows. For this the poor boys are bound to a block so tightly that they cannot make the least movement. The master or his assistant, using a small hooked knife, sharpened on both edges, makes an incision under the skin and out again at intervals of half an inch. These parallel incisions are continued in a long line or chain of identical scars.

Each tribe has its own pattern, to which these incisions conform. As a rule they begin on the nape of the neck, running in two lines down the back and then along the sides to the belly. The Buszis carry this tattooing to the farthest extreme, for their pattern of scars covers the whole of the back, runs together on the belly, and is then carried on up to the chest, where the converging lines fan out again. In addition to these tribal markings each Bush-master puts his own little sign manual, a closely guarded secret, by which all fellow sufferers can recognize one another in after life. To make the scars stand out as much as possible a juice of leaves and pepper is rubbed into the wounds while they are fresh; and with this the most painful part of the initiation into the Bush society is over. The boys are meant to show their manly endurance of pain at this first trial, but, as might be expected, neither the tattooing nor the making of the incisions is carried out without piteous cries from the victims.

When the scars have healed, these neophytes are led one by one into a river, where, with elaborate ceremonial, they cast leaves behind them, by which is meant that they cast their old selves behind them to be carried away on the stream. They leave the water as new persons and new members of the Grigri communion with new names. Their education as men now begins. They must learn to be silent and to obey. The strict discipline under which they live is never relaxed in the presence of their Bush-master as long as they live.

To harden them and inure them to exposure they sleep every now and then on the bare earth without any covering. They have to learn to endure hunger and thirst, but at other times they are well fed. They are taught the crafts of which every adult member of the tribe must be a master, such as farming, hunting, fishing, housebuilding, and also tribal history and the government and organization of the village and the tribe. They learn, besides, the secrets of the devil dancers and of their whole ritual symbolism, the secret signs of distress, warning, and recognition, and the mystery of reproduction. Thus, on the one hand, they lose their dread of all that hitherto has seemed incomprehensible and menacing, while, on the other, they are firmly linked up with this powerful club of men, which will henceforward play a greater part than all else in their lives. According to their bent and capacity they can advance in knowledge step by step. They are taught the rules, the steps, and leaps of the Negro dance and of the masked devil dances; they learn to walk on short stilts, which are constantly heightened until some at least qualify as stilt dancers on stilts over six feet high with their hands left free. The art of the drum and its language, as well as the harp and the horn is taught them too. Only the best are ever permitted to specialize in one particular branch. Those who are especially gifted or are the sons of chiefs are trained for the tasks of leadership they may one day need to take up, and the best pupils of all are brought up to be medicine men. Therefore in the long run only a few are accounted fit for the secrets of divination, of concocting "medicines," of prophecy and weather-making.

Once every year or two the devil brings his boys to the village; for this there is a special ceremonial; they are all dressed in the same fantastic dress, and are chalked white. Their faces are veiled with woven bamboo fiber, so that parents are unable to recognize their own sons in the long line of white figures dressed alike. The boys then perform their dances and show what they have learned. But the most important part of it is that the devil is once more loaded with offerings. After a few hours the whole grotesque company retires again into their Bush.

When six or seven years have been spent in this way the great day comes when the boys finally return to their village. If one of them happens to have died his mother finds a jar of rice at her door on the night before his hoped-for return. This is the first and only news she will ever have of the fate of the son whom she sent into the bush years before. Now she knows that he will not return, and, taking the jar, she leaves the village and stays away until the rice is finished, by which time the festival of the breaking up of the Bush will be over.

When the hour of the boys' return draws near the women dance through the village singing, "I hear a noise from the Bush, but I don't know what it is." The men go out to meet the approaching youths, and when the ecstasy of the women has reached its climax the devil, led by the Bush-master, who now makes his appearance openly for the first time, enters the village, singing as he did for the opening ceremony. Following him, as his tail, come the youths, crouching one behind the other, hidden for the time by cloths joined together and held up by the men of the place. The women all flee away in fear until the company has reached the market place, where all the youths, disguised as little devils, crouch close together in a long line with bent heads. The women now draw near, and the devil makes a lengthy report through his spokesman, dances, and performs magic. The youths dance, and so, lastly, do the fathers, who once again make presents to the devil and this time to the Bush-master as well. The chief officially takes back the youths from the Bush-master and releases him from his responsibility, after thanking him for his services.

The devil, however, retreats once more into the Bush with his pupils. There they take off their devil dress and put on the clothing brought them by their fathers. They then form a long line with their backs to the camp, which for so long has been their home. They sing, but may not turn their heads, while behind them their devil clothes, their huts, and all they possessed in the Bush go up in flames. The past is over, and no earthly memento which might entice them back into the past must survive. For this reason they are conducted back to the village by quite another road, and if possible to the other end of it. Once more they sit in the market place, and now it is they who receive presents and play the leading part in dance and merrymaking until nightfall. Not until dark may they leave the market place, taking their presents with them, and as new persons and full-grown men of the tribe return to their fathers' houses.

Such is the nature and practice of the secret West African Gri-gri club, as I got to know it among the Buszis.

Besides the Gri-gri Bush of the men there is also the Bundee

Bush of the women, which in principle is after the same pattern. The girls undergo similar incisions with a razor-sharp knife and are tattooed with stars, garlands, and other often very pretty designs on the belly, breast, and back. They learn to dance and sing, and are prepared for their future duties as wives and mothers. Rather surprisingly, no means are neglected for fattening them, as they thus correspond to the Negro ideal of beauty and command a higher price in the marriage bargain, which usually follows immediately on their release from the Bundee Bush. Their festal return from the Bush is a delightful scene; their hair is elaborately dressed, their dress and adornment are of a pleasing extravagance, and they dance as a rule to perfection.

And now smallpox had invaded a Gri-gri Bush of a village in Busziland; and the alarm and excitement of the mothers whose sons were in the Bush, but of whose fate—and whether or not they had succumbed to the plague—they would know nothing for years, could well be understood. When, with the chief and the utterly desperate and bewildered medicine man, I penetrated to the Bush, I found eighteen of the twenty-two boys seriously ill. Those who were still unaffected had in their terror withdrawn to a distance and left their unfortunate companions to their fate. So there they lay in the blazing sun, covered with pustules, in some cases confluent, forming large septic ulcers, upon which flies had settled in hundreds. Some of the boys could scarcely move for the agony they were in. Others had crept under a wretched palm-leaf shelter to find shade, whimpering for water they were unable to swallow. They lay uncared for in all their dirt and filth. No one had dared to touch them, and so it was a true deliverance for them when all day long we bandaged, washed, and tended them, put together beds with mosquito curtains, and soothed their

110

pain. I have rarely been rewarded with such thankful looks as I was that day. I could not stay on there myself, but I left one of my orderlies behind. In spite of all we could do not all the mothers saw their sons again, but when I returned to the village and they all crowded round me crying bitterly, I was able, with the Bush-master's consent, to tell them before I left that I had seen twenty-two youths in the Bush. Glad to know that all of them were at least still living, the poor women then let me go.

It seemed to give my black colleague, the medicine man, special satisfaction that I was as helpless as he in face of this outbreak of smallpox. The admission that even my power had limits lost me my nimbus of omnipotence, but gained me the medicine man's esteem as a man and a colleague. The hatred which the superior white intruder had drawn upon himself by undermining their prestige vanished when they found that there were sicknesses which put us on the same level of competence or of incompetence. And as I did not utterly condemn their methods of treating sickness, but was in fact, to their great astonishment, eager to acquire what they had to teach, I succeeded by degrees in winning their confidence.

For example, at Deseba, the home of my cook, Massa, I spent hours talking with the keenest interest to a medicine man who seemed to be as old as the hills. It was the first time I had ever entered the dwelling of a witch doctor such as he, and I was not a little astonished to find myself in a regular museum. The walls of the small and ancient house were thickly hung with moldering and rusty objects. Old swords, spears, bows, knives, "medicines," flasks, and any number of other things were suspended from the roof, and the floor was so crowded with jars, pots, and calabashes that there was only a narrow passage to the hearth and couch.

The Negroes hung back in awe, and no one except the chiefs dared to enter. Even Massa, who as interpreter was compelled to come in, would rather have stayed outside. Yet the toothless, bent, and gray-haired old man was delighted to have found some one to show his collection to. He was full of eagerness as he told me that all these things had belonged to the great men of the place from its earliest days. This was the sword with which a celebrated warrior had fought Denunnden. With that spear he had been slain. This was the first flintlock captured by the town. There hung the panoply of the famous chief, Salifu, and this medicine had already killed ten men. The old man's enthusiasm grew as he went on, and I could not get over my astonishment at all I saw and heard.

The things he showed me must have been very old indeed; some were very primitive in the way they were made and in their decoration; others of chased silver, inlaid with gold, ivory, and rare woods, were works of art of great beauty, even though they too were black with age and moldering away. The medicines had dried to a hard paste, swords and spears were eaten away with rust, leather and skins were rotting.

The finest piece of all was a three-foot-long horn, carved from an elephant tusk. On one side a wonderful devil's mask was carved in relief on the ivory, which was brown with age. I was so enraptured by this horn that I could not refrain from asking whether I might buy it. I knew very well how tactless my request was, but the horn was so original and curious that I could not help myself. The answer I got surprised me more than everything I had been shown.

"*Loketa,* the horn is very old, many years older than all the rainy seasons that you and I and our fathers put together have seen. It comes down from the time when there were still

112

elephants here in Deseba, and men who could carve their tusks with a knife. Such times I never knew even as a child. Its sound, too, is so loud that it can be heard in Monrovia." (About two hundred and fifty miles away.)

"It may be as old as you say, Finjah," I replied, "but its sound can never carry as far as that."

"*Loketa,* you do not know that. It is only blown in war and when this town is in danger. Anyone of Deseba who is in Monrovia when this horn is blown will hear it, not with his ears but in his heart, and then he will know that he must go to the help of his town. If this horn were missing from the town, then all of us who were in foreign places would be as orphans, as chickens who can no longer hear their mother's call. Do you believe me, *Loketa?*"

I was silent for shame, and when he went on my desire to buy the horn seemed even more reprehensible. "When you came to us the chief, Kuke, said to you the first day, 'The town and everything in it is yours, for you are our guest.' If now you say that you wish to have the horn, then I must let you have it, because it is yours, however it may grieve my heart."

I hope the old man guarded the horn for his town for many years to come.

We then squatted round the embers of his hearth until late at night, talking shop, and little by little I got a very good idea from him of the methods of healing practiced by the medicine men. Later on we even got so far as swapping medicaments, and of course he was particularly interested in anaesthetics, but I could not give him any samples of these. What he gave me were pressed leaves, pieces of bark, and precise descriptions of the trees the leaves of which were used for their specifics, and also recipes for the making of their medicinal drinks.

113

I carefully kept them all, hoping that later they might be of scientific value to some botanical gardens, but unfortunately the whole collection was eaten by ants before I got home, so that the old man was not after all deprived of his precious secrets any more than of his ivory horn.

By the time my stock of serum was exhausted I had, I thought, arrested the worst of the smallpox menace in this area, and so I returned to Vonjama. In many cross-country journeys up and down Busziland I had vaccinated over eighteen thousand persons and treated about three hundred cases, besides attending to various other matters of hygiene.

And now, just as I was on the point of returning to Bolahun, news came that smallpox had broken out farther to the south in Gisziland and was once more threatening to spread to Bolahun. I was almost in despair. To try to combat such an epidemic singlehanded in these vast areas of virgin forest was so utterly hopeless. It was like mending a leaky barrel.

However, on I went with my trusty boys over the near-by French boundary to Macenta and from there to Queckedou to beg for serum, and then hastened back as fast as I could to my own land of the Giszis. I found it very hard to turn my back on the warm hospitality of the French and the wonderfully civilized life of their well-administered settlements. When I left the fine, open, parklike country of Guinea and crossed the wide Makonna, which parts it from the primeval forest of Liberia, I felt an aching desire for beauty and civilization now that I had seen how possible it was to live with taste and dignity even here in the heart of Africa.

For the first time the depressing thought came to me that for me, as a German, there was no spot in the whole of this continent where I could exist except as a guest. Everywhere I was a stranger, and all I did was done for strangers. But,

114

after all, I had of my own free will chosen the forests of a foreign land; I had deliberately given up home and its cultivated life and could not now complain. It was merely that these gloomy thoughts had been brought out by the sudden contrast when I was compelled once more to follow the narrow winding trails of the forest and bush.

I had scarcely said good-by to the good food of Guinea and its comfortable means of travel than my old trouble assailed me with greater fury than ever. For two days I lay helpless, and now discovered that I was suffering from dysentery. But what could I do? I had to carry on with my job.

After six more days I had vaccinated only twelve hundred Giszis and dealt with forty cases. And with that I was compelled to regard my job as done, in spite of all gaps and shortcomings. I was at the end of my strength, and had to get back to Bolahun without further delay, even if I had not been summoned by urgent calls for help.

CHAPTER 6

My First Spell Ends

THERE WAS little rest for me on arrival at Bolahun. Once again work had accumulated during my absence. To start with, Jutta, in order to pay for the current expenses of building the hospital town, had been busily searching out cases for surgical operation and taking payment in advance in rice and oil. Forty patients presented their advance tickets, some of them over two months old. These cases must, whatever happened, be dealt with immediately. Besides these there were all the undiagnosed sick, who since they could not be treated until I came back had been waiting patiently for me in the old hospital town. Nor was this all, for the nuns, to a woman, were ailing, and one of them was dangerously ill with acute diarrhea. She gave me much anxiety for four weeks, until at last she was through the worst. The monks were not a great deal better off.

In these circumstances I had little time left over for attending to my own cure, unless I meant to be snowed under. As it was, in spite of my utmost diligence, I should never have got through if the long-awaited assistant from Europe had not turned up at long last. There he stood one day on my veranda, like a messenger from another world, tanned, brisk, abounding with health and energy, in a brand-new rig-out, with immaculate boots, and his hair smartly cut. How could a man look so shamelessly healthy? He never told me what he thought of me—pale, lanky, cadaverous, wearing a torn

116

shirt with buttons missing, and with hair cut in ridges by Massa. Anyway, solitude and the crushing pressure of work were at an end. The "white medicine man" had got a helper, so now all demands could be met. Dr. Krueger was a good fellow and we remained the best of friends, even after our ways had parted, until his tragic death.

First of all, I could take the opportunity of getting well again. I already looked forward to the time when we should all three be working in the hospital together, but before I was quite fit to return to duty Jutta got blood poisoning in the leg. It was a bad moment, and I began to despair. At last the clouds lifted. The nun who had been so seriously ill had recovered, Jutta was on her feet again, and I too had got my strength back, and now we were in good trim for the dry season and could meet its expected stream of patients in full force. The operations paid for in advance had all been worked off, and we faced the major campaign unencumbered.

If only I could have got the hospital town completed before this, but the final stages had been much slowed down. The rainy season had shown that we had made many mistakes in the layout of our surface water drainage, but the worst thing was that we ran into unforeseen difficulties with the roads leading to the place. We had to construct dams and drain swamps before we were done.

So it was towards the middle of the dry season before "Loketahun" was finally ready for occupation. From the hill on which the chief's house stood, one looked down on sixty houses, with a palaver house, laid out in wide streets round a fine square. It was a proud and happy moment when at last I saw before my eyes what I had conjured up out of nothing. I knew every stick and stone, and every corner reminded me of difficulties met and overcome. Now it was finished, and the

117

day for the sick to move in and for the inauguration ceremony could be fixed.

I therefore told the chief that he might allocate the houses and that the sick might get ready to move in, so as to avoid a great commotion when the day came. The result of these instructions was very typical of the natives. Not one of them moved a finger. Somehow they could not believe that the houses were really meant for them. But when a practical joker announced that the old hospital town would be burnt to the ground that very evening, with every one who was still in it, there was a wild stampede for the new town. They took to their heels with bag and baggage and never stopped to look behind them. They had no time or strength for more, and by nightfall they sat beaming with joy amid all the clutter, with no beds, fires, or any sort of comfort. When I made my evening round their faces shone with triumph. "Now burn away as fast as you like—we're safe!"

The inauguration itself was a genuine native festival. The whole population assembled in the square of the new town. I made the usual speech for such occasions, and announced certain rules and regulations to which the chief's approval gave the force of law. The chief next spoke and thanked not only me, but the workmen, and lastly one of the foremen made a short speech.

Then the festivity broke out with the earsplitting racket of several native bands. On the instant all sickness vanished from this city of the sick. Their exultation and delight were so infectious that I could not help distributing a hundred-weight of kola nuts among the people, just as if I had not already spent far too much of my own money on the scheme. Then towards evening the cow, dedicated to the occasion, was slaughtered, divided up, and devoured, to the accompaniment of much palm wine.

Until long after midnight the clamor and the music and the dancing could be heard from my hill, where we were holding another great festivity of our own. We had sent to French Guinea for some champagne, for I had just had a long-awaited cable from home, and was now engaged to be married; and this, on top of having got through the inauguration ceremony successfully, regained our health, and made good progress with the work, was good enough reason for dining in evening dress at a table laid to suit the occasion. We wanted to forget for once that we were far from civilization in the heart of darkest Africa. For this reason we had asked to be spared the customary visits of singers, dancers, and devil dancers. It was a day when we could do without them in spite of the interest there always was in comparing the music and dancing of the different native tribes.

I never ceased to wonder at their astonishing feats of music. Often boys or girls would play and sing all day long with only brief pauses. Dancing nearly always went on at the same time, and the more furiously they danced, the louder and wilder grew the music. Usually three or four voices, at least, sing polyphonically and are wonderfully harmonized. As in the well-known American Negro quartet, each sings his own tune and yet the whole blends in a most pleasing sound. Although they go in a great deal for syncopation, the rhythm is clearly marked; sometimes, even, the singers sing in syncopation only while the dancers keep the strict time with their rhythmical *"M-m-m—m-m-m."* One singer leads off with a song of five or ten words which are repeated over and over again. The other singers fit their voices to it and fall in, canon fashion. And so it goes on until the sign is given to stop. The tunes of

119

all songs are very alike and make use of a very small scale. They begin on high, long, and stressed notes and end, contrary to our practice, on low, short ones, without, as it were, stress or emphasis, slowly fading out.

As the sound and the rhythm are all-important, the words as a rule are very commonplace; they are adapted to the purpose of strolling musicians who expect to be well paid by those for whom they sing. This is the sort of thing they would sing for me in front of my house: *"Loketa hoho, loketa hoho,* you are a rich man. You are a great chief. No one has better medicine. You give us much money. We thank you and go." A song of this sort can be adapted to anyone whom they desire to compliment. Occasionally, if a dancer wants to express something out of the common in mime, the singers underline it by the text of their song.

They sing to the accompaniment of drums of various kinds, or little rattles, bright metal clappers, and such like. Their best drum for sound is one that is shaped like an hourglass and stretched with skins which can be tightened or relaxed by the pressure of the arm holding the drum to the breast, and so give out notes of varying pitch. They attain real virtuosity with these drums and can even play tunes on them.

Their most beautiful instrument is undoubtedly the fanga, a kind of lyre made from half a calabash which gives the resonance, and with strings of bamboo of different lengths strung across the prongs of a fork fixed to the calabash. The player of this stringed instrument sings to his own accompaniment; there is no dancing to it. The words are more important than the music; the fanga merely provides a musical accompaniment, rather like our songs to the lute. The real artists of the fanga are minstrels, who, as in Homeric times, celebrate the battles and heroic deeds of famous chiefs. But

A recent photograph of Dr. Junge with his wife and daughter

Entrance to the magic grove of the Gri-Gri Society, Gota

Girls from the bush, painted with chalk, resting after dancing

Native drummers

This devil's special trick is to grow enormously tall and then, in a flash, to shrink to nothing

Floods on the river

Women working, Bolahun

Harbor and street in Monrovia. Custom House is at the foot
of the hill

New building for hospital at Cape Mount

Educated Negroes at the opening of the Cape Mount hospital

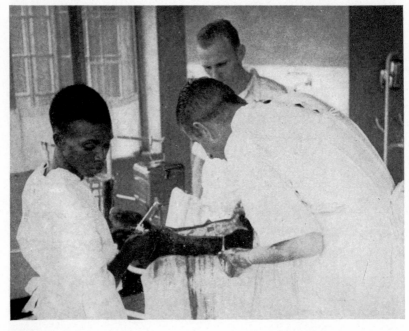

Dr. Junge performing an operation for elaphantiasis

even more popular with the Negroes, who are too much inclined to merriment to be greatly taken with history and tradition, are the folk songs sung by the fanga players. As examples here are literal translations I jotted down of a drinking song and a love song:

> Bring in palm wine!
> But see that it is fresh.
> We are very thirsty.
> We have conquered many enemies.
> No one is stronger than our chief.
> If we drink palm wine
> We are full of courage.

> When I bought you, you were a fine woman
> And you loved me very much
> And cooked a good rice for me,
> And I loved you very much too.
> Now you make up to others
> And cook rice for another.
> I shall get my money back from your parents,
> Or else you must be my good wife again,
> Because I love you much.

The themes of their songs—wine, courage, and the passing of love—in which the Negroes of the forests express their joys and sorrows are not so very alien to us. Also with the talent for singing and music it is much the same as with us; many think they are called, but few are chosen. The really good lieder singers among the Negroes are as rare as the delight in music and dancing is common.

Their way of dancing is far closer to the root idea of danc-

121

ing and leaping than ours is. They dance from the exuberance of animal spirits, not from conventional motives; consequently their dancing is entirely lacking in elevation and dignity. It is a wild and unrestrained leaping and jumping which exercises the whole body and recalls at first sight—if the comparison is not too far-fetched—the Tyrolese clog dancer.

They never dance in couples, and the sexes never dance together. The men form a semicircle round the musicians, and each man dances where he is, swinging his arms and stamping his feet, with his body bent forward while he performs his Charlestonlike steps. Suddenly one of them jumps forward out of the semicircle and performs a fresh dance with the wildest leaps and all the art and abandon of which he is capable. The music keeps pace with the dancer's ever-wilder tempo. The other men of the semicircle dance in harmony with their leader, whom they encourage with rhythmic clapping or with short, wild cries. The tempo and the frenzy rise faster and higher until the leader suddenly ends his *pas seul* with a succession of astonishing steps, and then leaps back into the circle to the applause of his fellows. Soon another takes his place in front and tries to outdo his predecessor's exploits. And so it goes on until no one else wishes to take the leading part. Then they form a long line, bending forward as though ready for a leap, and in close order circle round the players, stamping and uttering cries, or else, grappling each other low down from behind, vanish between the huts.

The ecstasy they work themselves up to by means of the monotonous repetition of their strongly rhythmical music is astonishing; so are the almost incredible feats of endurance it enables them to perform. A dance expressive often of all sorts of erotic suggestions may last without interruption from dusk to dawn.

122

The devil dances are quite different. They combine a dramatic display with an awe-inspiring demonstration of the power of the forest deities through the Gri-gri Bush fellowship, which is in alliance with them. The devils, who make their appearance in very handsome dresses of leather, bass, and hand-woven materials, are endless in number and variety. Every tribe has a whole array of different devils, to whom different magic faculties are ascribed. Some move and turn as though drawn on wheels, others increase and diminish their stature by as much as between three and six feet while they dance, apparently by raising or lowering their dance masks on sticks concealed within their wide bass robes. Still others whirl their inflammable bass skirts round at such lightning speed over a fire of blazing straw that they extinguish the flames.

Of all the exploits of the devil dancers the most impressive in my opinion is the dance of the devils on stilts. These devils dance on stilts which are over six feet high, but reach no higher than their knees. The stilts are loosely wound round with a brightly colored cloth and are furnished at the lower end with small bells which ring at every step. The upper part of the body is enveloped in a dark blue cloth with wide sleeves fitting over the hands; over this, on breast and back, they wear a sleeveless cape of pieces of leopard, beaver, and maned sheepskins, stitched on to red material adorned with cowrie shells. The face is concealed by a wire mask, and, lastly, the devil wears a conical hat, on the tip of which is a tuft of white wool. He holds in his left hand a clapper and in his right a short whip.

He enters the village with long swift strides to the wild strains of his own band and begins his dance. It is almost impossible to describe the amazing performances of this dancer, twelve feet tall. At one moment he falls stiffly forward, feet together, only to recover himself at the last moment by taking a long stride; at another, he stoops with his whole body stretched out parallel with the ground or he crosses one stilt over his shoulder and hops about on one leg. You think every moment he is going to fall, and the suspense is all the greater from knowing that these dancers are playing with their lives. A devil who comes a cropper has lost his power and so is mercilessly slain.

Everyone knows, of course, that the devil is a man; nevertheless the natives firmly believe that the dancer, when he dresses up, puts on besides his clothes a ghostly being of supernatural powers. If he falls it shows that these supernatural powers have forsaken him, and he must instantly be dispatched before he is possessed by some other magic powers which may this time be malevolent ones. As proof of this transformation of a human into a spiritual being, there is the inhuman speech of the devil, who talks in a high falsetto and sounds as though he had pebbles in his mouth; these incomprehensible utterances have to be translated to the people by his interpreter.

I found another very peculiar, and perhaps unique, devil among the Giszis.

The shrill sound of trumpets and the deep sound of moaning wind, produced by means of hollow vessels, announced the approach of a terrifying devil, who was reputedly invisible to women. Should a woman see him notwithstanding the penalty was death.

I was sitting at the time in front of my house, and I saw four Negroes proceeding slowly through the deserted village, blowing and drumming with all their might. At the first sound women and children fled in panic indoors and barred doors and windows so as to be sure of not catching so much as a glimpse of the dread portent. I waited in vain for the devil in person; and then my house surgeon, Njuma, who was with me at the time, explained that the devil did not in fact exist in corporal form. The women therefore would not be able to see him even if they did dare to take a peep through a chink.

I asked what, in that case, was the point of the performance and why they bothered.

"You must understand, *loketa,* that women have from time to time to be reminded of the superiority of men. Otherwise they get too uppish."

So that was the secret—nothing but a way of making doubly sure that women kept in their place.

Until a girl enters the Bundee Bush she is still a child and is treated as such. As soon as she leaves the Bundee Bush she passes as a rule straight into the hands of a man who probably bought her from her father as a small child, or else she remains for a short time in her parents' house until a man contracts to pay what the Negroes consider the very large sum of £12 for her. It is very seldom that the prospective son-in-law can pay up at once, and so at first he is in his father-in-law's debt. This long-term credit is really part of the game, because the sale of a daughter is a sort of insurance policy, in the sense that all financial obligations the parents now incur can, at least in part, be placed on other shoulders. The son-in-law is now involved in all major expenses, and he, of course, keeps strict account of each installment. As soon as he considers that he has paid off the purchase price in full he goes to his father-in-law for a final quittance. There is then a long palaver, and usually a pound or two extra must be paid before the son-in-law is allowed to go free. But if he is not pleased with his wife or if she is childless he can give her back and demand the repayment of all his installments at the earliest possible date. That, of course, is a severe blow to the wife's family, who endeavor by every means to avert the disaster. Daughter and son-in-law are both pleaded with in the hope of reversing the decision.

Rearing children is particularly arduous and difficult for native women, and makes their plight still more unenviable. There is no fresh milk. Flour and sugar are also lacking. Rice, fruits, and vegetables are all they have to feed their infants on. The children very early on contract malaria, with greatly swollen spleen, and this, with the unbalanced carbohydrate diet, gives little Negro children their familiar distended bellies. Infections by germs and worms follow, and so it is not surprising that the infant mortality rate is so shockingly high; every other child dies in its first year. The natives are themselves appalled by this and believe that they have found a remedy in prolonged breast feeding. They feed a little boy in this way for almost four years, and cling in desperation to this practice, even when they are told that towards the end their milk has scarcely any value as nourishment.

During all these four years the wife is taboo to the husband for fear of her milk prematurely drying up. But no one supposes that the man will live as a monk all that time, and so it is considered perfectly natural that he should, perhaps with his wife's assistance, look out for a companion to join his household. He may then decide to marry her as well or else send her away as soon as the time is up. If she has a child he will nearly always marry her in order to make sure of the child —always a much-desired possession. Should he not marry her there will be plenty of others who will be glad to take her with her child; children are a good investment—boys as workers and girls because of the price they fetch—and also they are the tangible guarantee of personal survival after death.

Thus it is that the Negro comes to have more than one wife, provided of course, that his means allow it. Polygamy is also the natural consequence of the ratio of women to men, brought about by the far higher infant mortality among male children. It is only chiefs and other wealthy men, with their hundred and more wives, who push this natural arrangement to the point of absurdity. Even so, it is an alternative to the socially unhealthy hoarding up of money in interest bearing investments in more competitive societies.

The head wife of a chief decides with rigid impartiality and not always according to the preferences of her lord which wife's turn it is and for how long she may cook for him and live with him. When her time is up this short-term favorite must make room for her successor, and it may be a year or two before her turn comes round again. During this interval the chief lends her to some worthy man who cannot afford to buy himself a wife or whom he wishes to bring into a more intimate personal relationship with himself. In either case a rent is paid. She then passes as the man's wife, with the proviso that the chief is regarded as the father of any children she may have. Unmarried men are a standing danger to the virtue of the wives of the place, and a wise chief in this way provides for his poorer sons, protects the virtue of his harem, ensures that his progeny shall be numerous, and enlarges his personal following.

Widows fall to the brother's share or to that of the deceased's legal heir, who may sell her if he likes. If a father finds no bidder for his daughter, as happens very seldom, he will make a present of her to some man of importance with whom he wants to be in closer relationship. A return present, at the recipient's discretion, takes the place of the purchase money.

127

Only those unfortunate women who have no children, however often they change husbands, and so return time after time to their father's house, are left unprovided for. They were the most grateful of patients when the cause of sterility could be removed, and their fathers were even more grateful.

With the exception of these unfortunate creatures, the women, although they work very hard, are never unprotected or left to fend for themselves. In return they have to do without any sort of personal liberty. They are sold according to the wishes of their fathers and husbands, and their husbands can return them or even sell them if they choose. If they wish to assert their own will they have only the weapons of Eve to rely on. How greatly these are feared even among Negroes is shown by the constant anxiety to shut women off from any sort of mental development and to keep them continually reminded of their inferiority.

For thousands of years the life of the Negro has developed on lines different from ours. Naturally all his social and moral conceptions are different also. They have led to laws which to us are utterly incomprehensible; even the ordinary native himself, if you discuss the matter with him, can give no idea of their original purpose.

One of these apparently crazy, but in reality very sensible, laws is concerned with the term "sister-in-law." The Negroes in this corner of the Liberian hinterland have no word for this relationship. Sometimes they call a sister-in-law "wife of my brother" and sometimes "my wife." It was not at all easy to unravel this confusion. The key to it is that, although the wife of a younger brother is forbidden to the elder brother, the wife of an elder brother is "my wife" with all the rights of marriage for the younger brother as long as he is unmarried. If he has

128

a wife of his own it is another matter; his sister-in-law is at once forbidden as the "wife of my brother."

This remarkable convention is explained by the relatively short life of the Negro. The parents might die before the children reached marriageable age; and then the eldest son might discharge his duties toward his younger brothers out of hand by making them his own slaves. But a younger brother had the right to his elder brother's wife, and the only protection against this lay in seeing that the younger brother was married as soon as possible, and so the elder did all he could to provide the younger with the money to buy a wife of his own. Domestic peace and happiness were therefore bound up with the care taken of the younger by the elder. A law of truly Solomonic wisdom.

It may be objected that, as in the Old Testament, he might simply have sold his brothers into slavery or his sisters into marriage. This was countered by yet another law which goes back to matriarchal times. Children count as direct blood descendants not of the father, but of the mother, and carry on the family of the mother. But since the mother, as a woman, is not legally competent, her nearest relation—namely, her brother—has the deciding word as to the upbringing and future of her children. Consequently it could only be their uncle on their mother's side who could sell them into slavery, not their father nor, after his death, their elder brother.

The last vestiges of matriarchy are also seen in the succession of the chiefs. The heir apparent is not the eldest son of the chief, but the eldest son of his sister by the same mother. But the succession is not strictly hereditary; all who consider they have any right by blood to the succession may make their claim before the council of the elders. The council then choose the man they consider best fitted, without being tied to the direct line of inheritance. This may seem in theory to be the ideal compromise between elected and inherited monarchy, but in practice the human weaknesses of self-seeking and corruption often prevent the best man from getting the job.

Earlier on I compared the natives of the Bolahun district with the men of the pre-Hallstatt Iron Age. Unfortunately we know too little of our primeval ancestors to say whether they had arrived at social laws which were as well suited to prevailing conditions and needs as were the examples I have given from the laws I found in operation among their Liberian "coevals." But the objects, whether utensils or ornaments, which have survived from their day show that they were superior to them in their standard of living, as well as in artistic expression.

The possessions of a Negro consist of as simple a house as you can imagine, made of pole, mud, and palm leaves, without windows and with a rush mat for a door. A fire burns day and night on a slightly raised mud hearth in the middle of the floor.

All you will find within are a few woven rush mats to sleep on, a stock of provisions, crocks of earth baked in the sun, a little clothing, some of the indispensable medicines, and a few simple tools. Artistic additions inside and out are very rare. Painting is almost unknown and is confined to tracing of the artist's own hand or a few childish silhouettes on the wall. Of plastic art there is nothing except clumsy ancestral effigies and the devil masks. In silver- and leatherwork they are far behind other African races. Their strong point is the weaving of cloth. But here too they are surpassed by their neighbors. One does not even get the impression that in their weapons and objects of daily use they have made any improvements since they first learnt how to work in iron.

I have often wondered why it is that in spite of their unquestionable liveliness of mind they have no new ideas, no flights of thought, and why their development came to a stop so long ago. Their freedom from the shackles of tradition, their openness to anything new, and their astonishing quickness at learning ought to have produced an indigenous civilization, just as their love of play and their delight in ornament and color ought to have flowered in a native art. Instead of this, they live on from generation to generation without developing any creative energy of their own.

The jungle must be to blame for it. For centuries the people have lived amidst swampy valleys and closely timbered hills. The great roof of leaves above them ties their gaze to the earth, and by restricting the sweep of their eyes hems in the flight of their thoughts. The luxuriant vegetation imposes a hard and endless battle in defense of their crops against the ever-encroaching bush. They may once have exulted in being able to win a living in their pitiless struggle and yet have lost touch with all they used to value before migrating into the forest; for most of the tribes of the Liberian hinterland are offshoots of the great Mandingo stock, which is of high repute in art and culture, as well as in trade and cattle raising.

When I visited French Guinea I saw this fine, proud race still inhabiting, without interbreeding with other races, a closed territory of its own. But what became of those Mandingos who, leaving the wide open country, ventured, whether of their own free will or not, into the virgin forest? In a few generations they descended to the level of the Ghandis, Buszis, and Giszis. Art and culture died out or were forgotten, and even they themselves became smaller, more slavish, less proud and self-reliant. The oppressive weight of the forest bowed their eyes to the earth, just as it transformed the mighty elephant of the open plains into the small forest elephant and the mighty hippopotamus into that remarkable species, the dwarf hippopotamus. Perhaps it is a law of nature that where the flora has uncontrolled sway, the greater fauna is stunted.

We Europeans, isolated in the forest, spent many a lonely evening in discussing such questions. We debated the problems which were always cropping up, and endeavored to unveil the mysterious laws of nature. These problems had an importance far beyond their intrinsic interest. They meant more to us than events in Europe and the rest of the world, news of which in all its clamorous urgency penetrated even to our retreat, though the tidal wave reached us after three or four weeks only as a ripple; we had no radio or air mail.

But our own world keeps its hold on us, however distant from it we may be, unless as monks or nuns we have said good-by to it for ever. And so it was with us. Jutta Kolbe had to leave us, as her mother had suddenly been taken gravely ill. It was a sad conclusion to our perfect collaboration. We two men, Krueger and I, were now left alone, and we had to have one of the nuns to help us with much of the daily work of the hospital which hitherto we had been spared.

Fortunately the dry season was drawing to an end, and the stream of patients began to diminish. Welcome as the dry season is to man and beast after the long rains, Africa, the land of extremes, cannot help overdoing the blessings of sunshine. The earth dries out and after several months without a drop of rain becomes yellow and hard; long cracks branching out in all directions seem to cry out in an agony of thirst. Leaves wither and fall; even the grass flattens out and turns to hay. The rivers shrink to trickles, many springs dry up altogether, and for weeks on end the sun scorches from the cloudless sky. The blazing heat, seldom fanned by a breath of air owing to the unbroken screen of forest, oppresses every living thing, and the smallest act demands a shocking expense of energy. The wood of doors and windows, swollen with moisture in the rainy season, is now as dry as tinder. The almost red-hot corrugated iron roofs strain and creak at every joint, and the mosquito netting lets undesired heat into the house while it keeps out what little breeze there may be. There is no end to the quarrels of the natives over the shrinking watering places, and the white men's tempers too become uncertain. When the sun declines at last and loses its power there is a brief hour of release in the cool of the evening until the night breaks in abruptly and swallows it up.

And now everyone is thankful to see the first clouds appear once more and to hear the first growls of thunder in the distance; they are the heralds of the transition period, which after long and violent thunderstorms leads into the wet season. I have never known such tremendous storms. The natives and their low, highly inflammable huts are protected by the tall forest trees. I never remember one of their huts being set on fire, and it was only occasionally that lightning tore out a bit of our roof, or a door, or a window frame.

When the rainy season sets in in earnest, then there is water and to spare. The springs abound, and rivers rise and rise until they reach the tops of the trees growing on their banks. The Negroes stay in their huts, work on the land ceases, and even the white medicine man has time to attend to his private affairs and amusements.

We now put our Klepper collapsible boat together and set off on voyages of discovery on the Kaiha. The Kaiha is one of the least known rivers of Liberia. Its source must be somewhere in the territory of the Buszis. It empties itself, as I later discovered, into the river Loofa, which reaches the sea at Little Cape Mount. The course of the Kaiha as well as that of the

Loofa, which is considerably over sixty miles in length, were then, and no doubt still are, very little known. Every map of the country gives them a different and quite arbitrary course. It was my great desire to explore the whole of the Loofa in our collapsible boat, but our experiences on the Kaiha showed us that this could be undertaken only by a well-equipped expedition with several boats, and for that we had neither time nor money.

The natives of the hinterland of Liberia are true landlubbers and have a horror of embarking on the water. But when a river is too wide to be spanned by their skillfully constructed rope bridges of lianas, they have to make rafts or dugouts, which with much shouting and alarm they use as ferries.

It is always a nerve-wracking experience to cross a river in this way with a long train of porters, as I often had to do on my travels. The first thing the ferrymen do is to retreat with their ferryboats to the farther bank, and then a long palaver begins over the price of the passage, carried on in shouts from one bank to the other. Taking advantage of the situation, the ferrymen make such shameless demands that on one occasion Massa in a violent rage threatened to pick them off one by one with his blunderbuss, so that at last they thought better of it and consented to come across. The porters and their loads have to be carefully apportioned to each crossing, and the boys shudder as they climb in. One clumsy movement will sink the boat, which is often only an inch or two out of the water. Not one of them can swim and they are thankful to get across in safety.

It is not surprising therefore that they have confined themselves to crossing the rivers, and have never thought of longer journeys upstream or down. Consequently any voyage on any of the rivers was a real voyage of discovery, and we could be sure that what we saw had never been seen before by mortal

eye since the beginning of the world. These primeval wilder-
nesses, which we came upon in our modern collapsible boat,
were a paradise of loveliness and made each trip an unforget-
able experience.

In the dry season the river sank so low that its bed was overgrown with scrub and reeds, and passage along it seemed in
places quite impossible; but during the rainy season one was
swept along by the current through the lower branches of trees,
which at low water filled the whole river bed with their network of grappling roots. The luxuriance of the forest itself is
far outdone by the almost unimaginable extravagance of the
growth in these river beds. Giant trees push each other into
the water and, losing their hold on the banks, sink half uprooted
into the river. They then grow on in a slanting or even hori-
zontal posture, partly die off, and throw up fresh limbs in a
new direction, entangled in mazes of lianas, which run up their
defiant garlands of a brilliance scarcely to be believed. Parasitic plants settle on the large overhanging branches and let fall
a tenuous sheet of root tendrils to the water, so that the boat
passes through what are actually curtains of roots. Seedlings
and even small trees strike root on rotting trunks afloat in the
water, which form islands of the decaying vegetation carried
down on the current and are anchored to the bank by coiled
ropes of fiercely luxuriating lianas. The sound of an ax or a
bush knife has never broken on this paradise nor a shot ever
disturbed it.

The animals have not learned to fear and flee from men, and
even our brightly painted collapsible boat, coming noiselessly
upon them, did not immediately frighten them away. Monkeys
of many kinds uttered cries in every tone from the trees, made
daring leaps to the other bank from overhanging branches,
stared at us in astonishment, or else raced each other through the

tree tops at the sight of such a portent. Herons stood in the shallows, ducks and water hens flew up, and flocks of wonderfully brilliant blue and yellow pheasants perched on the branches. Enormous creatures resembling pelicans flew away over our heads, beating the air with powerful wings, and we saw numbers of other birds which were quite unknown to us. Now and then big game of some sort could be heard in the undergrowth, or a hippo took to the water with a great splash. Once, when we were hugging the bank, one of these hideous beasts suddenly emerged from the jungle with its great elephantine skull reaching out over the water and gave us a fright by plunging in almost on top of us. Then there were the inevitable snakes lying unobserved along low-hanging branches, from which they glided silently, to swim in graceful curves through the water. Crocodiles of alarming size basked on bare trunks in midstream and vanished noiselessly and without hurry at our approach. We were always loath to shatter the peace of this paradise, but we had to shoot in self-defense when our way was barred in a narrow channel by one of these horny-hided monsters.

What with one thing and another, lovely as the scenes were through which we voyaged, it was very often no small task, and not without danger either, to explore the fifteen miles or so of the river that were within our reach. In places the tangle of foliage which dipped into the water was so dense that once carried into it on the current we did not know, particularly on our first trips, where we were getting to or how we should ever find our way out again. There we sat in a thicket of lianas and leaves and branches, struggling with the help of the current to fight our way on.

Once when we were driven in this way into a tree top we found that it was swarming with ants. We had to paddle like mad to get away. We were being devoured by them all the time, and even when we got clear we had to make for the bank at full speed to rid ourselves and the boat of the swarms we had already taken on board.

Another time a long snake fell like a thick black skein into my lap. In our passage through a tree Krueger, who was in the bow, must have shaken it from the branch on which it was dreaming or dozing. Fortunately it was even more alarmed than I was, so I was able to snatch it up in my panic-stricken grasp and heave it overboard before it had time to think of biting me. Crocodiles too, plunging into the water almost on top of us just when we had got our boat stuck fast, were also far from pleasant.

We had taken for our motto "Once capsized as good as eaten!" and we were correspondingly cautious. Nevertheless, it was hardly to be expected that our daily voyages would not one day end in some dramatic disaster.

Tree trunks were always a very awkward obstacle. If we could not push them under water and pass over them, we were forced to come alongside and after hauling the boat over embark again on the other side.

On our last journey we ran into just such an obstacle. But in this case the trunk was so low in the water that it was awash and consequently very slippery, and what with this and the rapid current great skill was called for in dragging the boat across without falling in ourselves. When we had successfully brought off this acrobatic feat, our next task was to haul the boat alongside the trunk against the force of the current, to enable us to embark once more.

In my desperate efforts to counteract the current by pulling on the painter, my bare feet slipped on the smooth and slimy surface and I fell backward into the water. As I let go of the painter the boat naturally was swept away on the current, and Krueger, who was holding on to it by the stern, was caught completely off his guard, and took a header on the other side of the trunk. When I rose to the surface I was swept against the side of the trunk again, but Krueger was carried downstream behind the boat. He stopped at the next overhanging tree and the boat at the next but one.

After we had both reached the bank hand over hand in the best gymnasium style, and had a good laugh over our baptism in the Kaiha, we turned our thoughts to the salvaging of our boat. But to our consternation the boat was gone, in spite of the two air cushions, which ought to have kept it afloat. If it had sunk, it could have been only from running against a branch and so capsizing. The force of the current must then have driven it under in spite of the air cushions.

So there we were, soaked to the skin and shipwrecked, with nothing left us but a paddle and a half, and the forest all round us. All we could do was to mark the scene of the disaster and then find our way home barefoot.

After a few whiskies plans were made for raising the sunken boat. There happened to be a party of Mandingos in Bolahun at that very moment on their way from French Guinea. Mandingos are more at home in the water than our Liberian backwoodsmen, and these fellows agreed to help in the salvage operations in return for suitable payment. Next morning, while I put in my day's work at the hospital, Krueger set off with ten of these six-foot-six giants to find our boat. When they got back in the evening they said they had found it, but it was caught fast in some branches under water; and they had been too tired to get it free. They were going back next day. In case it might be swept away they had bound it to the spot by a spell.

Next day, however, was a feast, which as strict Moham-
medans they were bound to observe. It was not until the third
day after the disaster that I set off with the salvage party, leaving Krueger on duty. We had scarcely started when we came
in for a regular forest rainstorm, which soaked us to the skin.
Even on the river bank, where we hoped that some thicket
would give us better protection, we had difficulty in finding a
spot where we could light a fire. We succeeded only after
several vain attempts, and then the boys, who were shivering
with wet and cold, were able to warm themselves. After this
they scattered in all directions, shrilly chanting Mohammedan
prayers to drive away all crocodiles and snakes. Then they
jumped into the river without fear, convinced that the might
of Allah, invoked by their prayers, had driven off all dangerous
beasts. But possibly it was the noise of their prayers, and the
continual shouting and hallooing resounding over the water,
which scared off all inhabitants of that peaceful paradise.

The whole salvage party then climbed into a tree which
stood up to its top in the water with its branches reaching out
towards the farthest bank. A long pole was pushed straight
down into the swiftly flowing river just where the boat was
supposed to be firmly wedged. They looked just like black
hens as they sat crouching on the branches before diving one
after another, guided by the vertical pole, in an attempt to
release the boat. They came to the surface again twenty or
thirty yards lower down, shouted out the results of their diving
operations and reached the bank in a quick crawl.

I had always rather fancied myself at diving, and when they
still had no success I concluded that the fault as usual lay with
the native's lack of technical accomplishment. So I decided to
dive myself. Even if I had no success either, I should at least
spur them on to greater efforts. To avoid being swept away by

139

the current, I followed their example in submerging head first with the pole to guide me. The current, however, very soon turned me right over, and I had to come up again at once. When I emerged beside the pole, I was greeted with smiles of pity by the boys squatting on the branches and was forced for my own credit to try again.

This time I did better, though I never reached the boat. I got well down, but was soon entangled in sticks and branches, lost hold of the guide pole and tried to take advantage of the current. I soon found myself in a regular thicket and had the crazy feeling that I was tree-climbing under water. Suddenly I got free and shot like a rocket to the surface. My exploration had been somewhat prolonged, so I was greeted with a loud shout of welcome. They were all convinced I had reached the boat, which for truth's sake I had to deny.

Hoping for the proverbial luck, I made a third try, this time with one of the boys. I could dimly see him winding like a serpent into the depths without a check, whereas I suddenly bumped into something with my head. After that I gave up my arboreal feats under water. Later when the boys pulled out the pole, and I saw that its length below the surface was little short of eight yards, it was obvious that my efforts were doomed to failure from the start. I had never in my life dived to such a depth.

I must have been a strange sight, with my white skin, a towel round my shoulders, a helmet on my head, and a pipe in my mouth, sitting by the fire in the subdued light of the forest and the pouring rain with these magnificent fellows whose bodies might have been carved out of ebony. I felt that my light skin was positively hideous and that I was the only naked person there.

After a short break for warming up they went on diving

140

indefatigably, until at last one of them came up and said that the boat had given a lurch when he pushed it. We saw nothing of it, however, on the surface.

Now that they were starting on such tales I felt sure they were losing interest, and I was confirmed in my opinion when the next boy to dive swore on his return that the boat was no longer there. If it had in fact got free, it must have come to the surface.

But to my astonishment they now began to search among the trees downstream. Had they not been lying after all?

Suddenly the boat was seen careering along far ahead. At that hell broke loose. With frenzied shouts and in wild excitement they raced along the bank in pursuit or plunged headlong into the river as though it might once more escape us. How I ever followed them through the forest, barefoot and naked, I shall never know.

And so the runaway was captured. As we had firmly lashed all our equipment in case of accident, it was captured complete. Even our shoes and the missing half paddle had gotten caught in the boat.

Full of pride and with triumphant song these fine fellows bore back to Bolahun the prize they had fought for so valiantly. They were the heroes of the day, greeted on every hand with amazement and admiration. But they modestly waved thanks aside. "Allah be thanked. It was His will." They gladly accepted the promised reward and then continued their journey in the highest spirits.

We had now had enough, for the time being, of our voyages of exploration on, and in, the forest rivers of Liberia. Also the eighteen months for which I had contracted were drawing to an end. Krueger would now be left to himself, and therefore it was imperative that the nun who helped in the hospital

141

should be thoroughly trained, and everything possible done, now while there were two of us, to lighten the load which would fall so much more heavily on one.

I had now been a year and a half in the forest as the great magician and white medicine man. Errors and failures had not been spared me, but all the same the hospital had made progress and was, indeed, a different place. The sick were well housed in Loketahun, and our labors had at least earned the trust of the natives, who came to us as patients in ever-increasing numbers.

Was I now, as I had originally planned, to bring this African episode to an end with the end of my engagement and return to Europe? The monks offered to renew my appointment and I had received an offer from Cape Mount Hospital, on the coast. Even the Liberian Minister of Health at Monrovia, Dr. Fuszeck, had invited me to pay him a visit and stay on there.

Europe had lost all charm for me. I resolved to remain in Africa, and of all the offers made to me the one that attracted me most was that I should stay on here in Bolahun and continue my work in the lonely mission station in the depths of the forest.

I therefore signed a new agreement with the monks, and then made ready for the great expedition straight through the uninhabited Kongwa forest, which I had already skirted on my elephant hunt, to the coast. There I was to board the ship which would take me on furlough to Europe.

CHAPTER 7

Black and White

ONCE MORE the time had come to enlist porters and get ready for a trek through the virgin forest. This time the equipment of my little caravan was governed by the fact that I was not returning immediately to Bolahun, and so I could sell or give it away on reaching the coast. Everything, therefore, was of the simplest. Twelve strong and healthy porters were selected who were prepared to accompany me on the journey of over two hundred miles. Massa, whom I had promised in return for his trusty service to take with me to Germany, said good-by to his wife and his women friends, and then we were ready to set off.

The monks, Dr. Krueger, and a large concourse of patients saw me on my way with great acclamation and cries of *"Isser ho."* I had to promise over and over again that I would not fail to return. Gradually one by one they all fell away until at last Krueger too turned back to bear the whole burden alone until my return.

It was a wonderful feeling to be free of responsibility and to turn my face once more towards home and civilization. Somehow my high spirits spread to the porters, and so we went singing and exulting on our way southwest through the forest.

It took us once more to Kailahun, the native place of Fafulekolli, Massa, and Momo. I was expected and so was welcomed as an old friend. Mussa was now chief and gave me a proud greeting as became his new dignity. The great funeral ceremony for Fafulekolli had taken place some months before

143

and nothing now was seen of his house, where I had last seen him alive, except the flat stones laid round the site as a memorial. With that, however, the debt of veneration had been paid. Washing was spread on the stones to bleach, and a bitch suckled three puppies on his grave. Nobody seemed to find anything strange in that, and so I had no excuse for my few moments' silent contemplation of the resting place of the great Negro prince. In fact Mussa thought my visit to the grave slightly uncalled for. It was obviously much more important that I should hear of his latest hunting expeditions. The burden of the chieftanship had not prevented his going off hunting in the forest. He showed me a little chimpanzee measuring about two feet when sitting down which he had captured alive and specially prized. He gave it me to remember him by. I was delighted to have the lively little fellow, even though it meant having a traveling cage made for him and taking on an extra porter.

Kailahun was the last place of any size on this side of the uninhabited Kongwa forest belt which separates the interior from the coastal region. From now on it would not be easy to find our way. Mussa with some of his men gave us one day's escort to a small village on the confines of his territory. From there a little-used trail was said to lead through the forest to the first village of the Gola Negroes on the other side. The chief told us to reckon on a four-days' march before coming to any human habitation. It did not enter his head that anyone ever lost his way or went in a wrong direction. I had to insist on his giving me a landmark or two, so that I could know we were taking the right course through the green ocean of trees. Then he accompanied us for one more short stage of our journey into the unknown, in case we took the wrong track where the trail forked, and then he bade us farewell.

The interminable forest swallowed the little troop of fifteen men who now followed the narrow path in single file.

In the depth of primeval forest, as on the sea or in the desert, I am always overcome by the almost crushing feeling of the infinity of nature. The insignificance of one's own existence is brought home to one when compared with the immensities of space or, as in the forest, with teeming life in all its myriad variety.

Here a paltry handful of two-legged creatures, like so many other animals, anxiously go their way amid centuries-old trees. Everywhere on earth their prescriptive weapon of reason has made them the lords of creation and developed their consciousness of their own ego to such a pitch that each one of them is convinced that his own life alone has meaning and importance. Full of this conviction they advance proudly into the jungle, and there they learn that they are no lords here, but mere nobodies whose living or dying means no more to the teeming luxuriance and lavish decay of nature than when a tree or even a leaf falls to the ground. The forgotten awe and humility in face of the omnipotence of nature, which they thought had been mastered, returns again to their hearts.

To lighten the boys' loads I had taken only a small supply of food, relying on game for supplying our needs. On the first day there was no trouble in bagging plenty. Massa and I kept half a mile or more in advance of the porters and as we made no noise we put up more game than we needed. Guinea fowl, pheasants, monkeys, and tortoises made up our bag, which we left on the track for the porters to pick up.

Once we came on the fresh spoor of the little dwarf antelope, the folintanga; whereupon Massa ran back two or three hundred yards and put two crossed sticks on the path to tell the caravan to halt. Our aim now was to shoot one of these gazelle-like creatures, scarcely twenty inches in height, the flesh of which is excellent. We took cover a few paces to one side of the path, and Massa, by stretching a grass between his fingers, imitated the long-drawn, plaintive call. After a few minutes a small buck suddenly appeared without a sound, like a spirit conjured up from the ground, and cautiously sniffed the air from the cover of a bush. It was an easy shot.

We could not expect the porters to add more to their loads, and so shooting was now abandoned in spite of abundant opportunities; as we had been on the march all day with only brief rests, we looked out early in the evening for a suitable camping place.

We found a small grassy clearing on a little headland formed by the bend of a fair-sized stream, and there we pitched our camp. Shelters of palm leaves were made in case of rain, and there was very soon a lively roasting and boiling over a number of fires.

Suddenly, however, two of the boys who had been having a look round in the neighborhood of our bivouac, came up to me in great excitement. *"Loketa,* there are the tracks of buffalo quite close. We must go!"

The reddish-brown African buffalo is the most dreaded of all the big game of the forest. It is the only beast that attacks human beings without being shot at. And when wounded it has been the end of many an unfortunate hunter. The boys' anxiety was therefore very natural, but I could not make up my mind to go in search of another camp just before dark. To pacify them I set off at once with Massa to follow the spoor. But we looked for it in vain, and also it very soon grew too dark to shoot.

So when I returned empty-handed to my apprehensive porters I had to fall back on magic. I had small stakes stuck into to the ground all round our camp and joined up with lianas, to which at wide intervals I attached leaves from my notebook, inscribed for greater mystical effect with my name. I explained that by this magic our bivouac was made invisible to any buffalo, and thereupon in full reliance on the great powers of the white medicine man they returned to their beloved occupation of eating and chattering.

When nothing was left of the game I had shot, we all lay down round the fire to sleep, tired out after a fatiguing day.

I could not have been asleep long when I was suddenly awakened by an appalling racket. Darkness, shouts, torrential rain, and thunder! Before I was fully awake everything fell in on top of me. I was buried under the palm-leaf roof and entangled in the mosquito net which had been stretched beneath it. Vivid lightning split the sky, followed by terrific bursts of thunder. Great limbs were wrenched from tree-tops and came crashing to earth with a shattering noise. The sound of the rain alone, whipping through the trees rose to a roar. Our fires were put out in an instant, and in the utter darkness we were more blinded by the brilliant flashes than enabled to see the utter destruction of our camp.

When at last I found my torch and got free of the entanglement of netting and branches, I collected my terrified flock with the aid of the light and much shouting. Tamba Foja, one of the boys, had been hurt in the foot by a falling branch, but the rest of us were safe and sound.

As long as the tornado went on and the lightning was close over our heads, we were helplessly exposed to the dangers of broken branches and falling trees. We could only crouch down in dumb endurance until after half an hour the storm eventually passed over.

There was now only the pouring rain. We had no protection from it. The palm-leaf shelters had gone, the blankets were soaked and far too heavy to stretch out over our heads, the temperature had fallen sharply, and lighting a fire to warm ourselves by was out of the question. Worst of all, the stream, in a bend of which we had encamped, began to overflow its banks. We sat with our feet in the water, and our baggage was wet through from below as well as above. Our camp had to be abandoned. All the baggage was carried up on to higher ground among the trees, and there we crouched down again with our teeth chattering, until at last towards morning the rain stopped and the sun broke through the trees, bringing light and warmth.

We were stiff and weary after a sleepless night, and first had to deal with the confusion all round us. We searched our camping place, now a marsh and covered with the wreckage of our shelters; we wrung out the blankets and hung them up to dry, and then with great difficulty got a smoky fire of wet wood to burn, made coffee, and sorted out the loads. Everything was wet, and what was spoilable was spoiled. The cartridges for my shotgun were wet too and had to be put out to dry round the fire. Tamba Foja's wound was unpleasant, but he thought he could get along in spite of it. I shared out two moist loaves —my iron rations—and waited until the sun was well up in the sky before telling the boys to pick up their loads; they were all the heavier for their wetting and the pace was slow.

The narrow trail was not always easy to find after the storm, and I had to rely on the compass more than usual. Towards noon we reached a rocky hill which was one of Mussa's landmarks. We were greatly relieved to know for certain that we were on the right track, and we stopped there for a rest.

As the soaked and dripping forest had been utterly dead in the morning, I made a little hunting trip here from our stop-ing-place, and we had the luck to run into a troop of monkeys. But, try as I would, I missed every shot. We returned to the bivouac in a very ill-humor and had to be satisfied with rice and palm oil, to which the boys added some edible leaves cooked as spinach. We ought by evening to have reached a considerable river, probably a tributary of the Loofa, where I had intended to camp for the night; but our pace was too slow, and when we had still not reached it by nightfall I decided to stop at a small clearing and spend the night there.

Warned by experience, the boys made stouter palm-leaf shelters, and while they did so I tried my luck once more. Again I only shot holes in the air. I did not discover what was wrong until we were sitting round the fire and discussing the day's events. My cartridges were all suffering from delayed ignition. The powder had clotted owing to the damp and did not explode as soon as I pulled the trigger. The consequence was that I was always shooting behind. Once more our meal was restricted to rice and palm oil, which, as our salt had all dissolved the night before, tasted very insipid.

Of course, now that we were well prepared for a downpour, not a drop fell. We had a good night's rest, and so set off next morning in better spirits. Very soon we reached the river we had been told of, but it was much too deep to ford and moreover it was running fast; the only way of overcoming this obstacle was to construct a raft.

A large heron did me the favor of remaining motionless until my delayed ignition cartridge made up its mind to go off. and the prospect of fresh meat put such heart into the men that they very soon built a raft of some logs which they found lying ready on the ground and which they lashed together with lianas. For paddles we had to use small leafy boughs. Two of the boys who were able to swim made the first crossing with me. Our narrow raft was flimsy and far from watertight; nevertheless we reached the farther bank undismayed. What surprised me most was that we bore up against the stream so well with our primitive paddles, that the rope of coiled lianas we dragged with us reached all the way across. We now lengthened it and hitched it to a stout tree trunk. With help of this cable and a crook cut from a forked branch the raft could be ferried to and fro across the river.

It had taken the boys surprisingly little time to fix up our ferry, but one boy and his load, besides the ferryman, was the utmost the frail raft would take, and, even so, cargo and passenger had to be very carefully stowed to avoid capsizing.

Disaster came with only the second crossing. For some reason the raft slowly sank on one side. The boy could not swim and in alarm he tried to correct the balance. He overdid it and the narrow raft went down on the other side. Half overboard, he managed to hold on to the outside log, but his load slid off and was lost to sight. It was good-by to rice, palm oil, cooking pot, and frying pan.

Attempts at salvage would of course have been useless. I was thankful that the boy had not gone as well. All loads were now roped with lianas so that if they went overboard we could haul them in on the rope.

After this we all got across without further mishap. The porter whose load was lost now had to take over Tamba Foja's, the boy with the bad foot. As a substitute for the missing utensils we had to make use of the basin which the porters had brought to hold the cooked rice for their communal meals always assuming that we had anything to cook. For the moment the long-legged heron dangling from the chimpanzee's cage was all we had in the larder.

By the evening, however, I had bagged two monkeys with

one shot. As I was shooting with the elephant gun, they were badly torn up. And neither heron nor monkey on a spit, without salt or garnishing can be recommended to the gourmet. But there was no help for it: monkey and tortoise were our principal food for the next two days. We once had the heart of a palm, cut from just below the tree's plume of leaves, as a vegetable. It is very tender and has a pleasant flavor, but a whole palm has to be sacrificed for one meal. A vegetable rather like asparagus is prepared by the Negroes from the young shoots of a prickly creeper.

And so in one way or another we managed to appease our rumbling stomachs; all the same, a shout of joy went up when at noon on the fourth day we came on an overgrown and abandoned rice field. That meant we were approaching human habitation. The prospect of procuring rice, the only food the Negroes regard as a proper meal, spurred us on. We found some banana trees on the rice field, and this made an end of fasting for Puck, the little chimpanzee.

Towards evening we were descending a hill. The trail was by this time wide and well-trodden; and when the men saw smoke in the distance they broke into wild howls of delight. Massa, in his enthusiasm, fired a salute of two delayed ignition cartridges.

Our horror and amazement were all the greater when on entering this longed-for village we found it completely deserted. We looked into the ten huts and saw that they must have been abandoned by their occupants only a few moments before. The fires were still burning and there was partly cooked rice in the earthenware pots, but except for a few mangy dogs lying in the sun and some cackling hens on the roofs there was no living creature in the place.

My boys accepted all this as a miraculous gift from heaven,

and in a moment they were sitting round the fires cooking for all they were worth to make up for the privations of the past days. When they even found a calabash of palm wine their enthusiasm rose to the highest pitch.

It was clear enough to me that the inhabitants had heard our exultant shouts and the two shots, and had fled in panic, expecting an attack either by angry bush spirits or a hostile Negro tribe. This great stretch of forest, which human beings scarcely ever traversed, was bordered on the east by the Gpesses, a tribe who even in those days bore the reproach of being cannibals on occasion. Perhaps the villagers had expected an onslaught from that direction. I felt sure they could not be far away, and I went with Massa along all the deserted paths around the village, calling out in the hope of persuading the terrified inhabitants to return. It was useless. Not one showed up.

I should have been glad enough to have gone no farther that day, and my porters were already settling in for the night. But there was the risk that the villagers might get help from neighboring villages and fall upon the "robbers" in the dead of night; and I dare not let that happen. So I decided to continue our journey as soon as the boys had eaten their fill. They were very reluctant indeed to set off again, but resigned themselves to it when they found that even the plea of Tamba Foja's terrible foot did not work.

Before leaving the village all loads were searched for objects which had been included by "oversight." Nothing but rice might be taken, and whatever else was found was laid down in a heap in the middle of the village. Then, when all the porters were on the march, I returned with Massa to the huts we had made free with, and left in each a fair payment for the provisions we had consumed and taken with us. I knew how swiftly news traveled in the forest, and I had no desire to be outlawed as a robber chief in the territory of the Golas and Vais, which we were now entering.

In spite of these precautions I was quickly given a very bad name. I had with me only brass shillings, which are good money in the hinterland of Liberia, but no silver shillings, which alone were accepted on this side of the forest. My reputation as a doctor had not penetrated to these parts, but I very soon had that of a passer of bad money, and I could buy nothing from the natives for the rest of our journey.

Consequently we were very soon in trouble again over the commissariat, and all sorts of diplomatic ruses had to be resorted to in order to wheedle provisions or quarters for the night out of the inhabitants before letting them see the color of our undesired brass shillings.

Soon I had an imposing procession of aggrieved creditors at my heels; I had promised to change the bad money for the coveted silver shillings in Cape Mount, my immediate goal.

Things being so, it was of course impossible to get porters for Tamba Foja, who was now quite unable to walk. Nor would he consent to be left behind with only brass money among a strange tribe. Once more we had to rearrange the loads in order to release two boys to carry the injured porter in a hammock. This reduced our rate of marching still further, and we were all relieved when we arrived at Jabacca, on Lake Pizo, the end of our journey on foot through the forest belt of Liberia. I could now lay claim to be one of the few Europeans who had ever traversed the trackless and unexplored region lying between Bolahun and Cape Mount.

There were black traders in Jabacca, on the edge of the great lake, acting as middlemen in the trade between white merchants and the natives; and at last I found people to come to my aid. I could buy oranges and other food on credit and,

153

above all, I could appease the clamorous throng of brass money duns. They also promised me two canoes large enough to hold my fourteen men and all our baggage, to take us across Lake Pizo, which separates the Cape Mount peninsula from the mainland.

The crossing of about twelve miles took us several hours, and landed us at Robertsport, which is the seaport of the peninsula. Cape Mount is a delightful spot. A narrow peninsula runs parallel to the coast from southeast to northwest, and is separated from the flat mainland by this extensive lake. At its northern end rise three peaks, between four and five thousand feet in height, clothed in dense forest. To seaward their wooded sides are rocky and precipitous, but on the landward side their descent to Lake Pizo is gradual. It is only on the north of the peninsula, where an extensive lagoon and a broad sandbank separates the lake from the sea, that the forest has been felled to provide an open site for some houses, which gleam in the sun. Robertsport, small and scattered, is situated on the edge of the lagoon, and its three thousand inhabitants live partly in native huts, partly in funny little shanties of corrugated iron, and partly in well-built, whitewashed houses. Natives of the Vai, Kru, and Gola tribes live in their own little settlements, separated from the Americo-Liberians, the descendants of those who once left Africa as slaves; between the two, European traders are established here and there along the edge of the lagoon. The white buildings halfway up the sloping hillside are the American Mission; and this was my destination.

We climbed slowly up, gaped at on all sides with undisguised astonishment, which was no greater than the astonishment of my porters at their first sight of the unbounded ocean. At last they could set down their loads and were given quarters in one

of the buildings which were such a surprising sight to them;
and I was taken charge of by the American missionaries.

The fatigue of my latest trek through the forest and the last
vestiges of my attack of dysentery were soon put right by the
good food provided by the ladies of the American mission; and
then I had to consider resuming my journey.

First I had to take leave of my porters, who had enjoyed their
days at Cape Mount as rustics enjoy life in great cities. Each
one was given a small sum on account and a credit note for the
greater part of their wages, which would be paid them on my
behalf by the monks at Bolahun. This roundabout method of
payment was necessary because they would infallibly have
spent their wages to the last penny on the spot and then have
arrived home empty-handed. They would then, as Negroes
always do after working for a white man, complain of the bad
pay, and never think of confessing that they had "blued" the lot.
Being well acquainted with this maneuver, I resolutely refused
to pay out a large proportion in ready money. Besides a parting
present, each boy received a headcloth for his wife, which
certainly not one of them would have thought of. Whether it
ever in fact reached its destination is, of course, another matter.
At last, after lengthy farewells and laden with many treasures,
they took the road home again. I myself had to get on to
Monrovia, and for this I chartered one of the large rowing
boats which were lying in the harbor. They belonged to a
German merchant.

These boats are from fifty to sixty feet long, resembling in
their build the boats carried on large liners, and they are perfectly seaworthy. The whole coastal trade of Liberia is carried
on with them and also the loading and unloading of ships anchored outside the reef. They are manned by a crew of twelve
hefty boys; and cargoes, often of astonishing tonnage, are

brought in several times a day over the reef which stretches in front of the river mouths or the entrances to the lagoons. Heavy seas breaking on this reef form a dangerous barrier in front of most West African ports.

The owner of the boat took the opportunity of visiting the capital, and had an awning put up in the stern. One of the more reliable members of the crew took the rudder and we set off with the good wishes of those who remained behind.

After we had safely crossed the dangerous reef a sail was run up, the rowers lay down in the shade of their seats, and the boat was borne gently southeastward over white-crested waves with the coast well in view. The glowing heat soon drove us from beneath our awning and we sat on the gunwale with our feet in the water, talking at length about our experiences of this strange land where the black man ruled. Meanwhile the Negroes made a fire on a sheet of corrugated iron and cooked their rice. Hour after hour went by, and it seemed that the mountaintops of Cape Mount would never let us out of their sight.

At last the night brought the longed-for coolness and a momentary freshening of the light breeze. We all felt the relief, and now, as we sped along more nimbly, Cape Mount at last sank into the darkness astern. The clear silvery sky and a silence broken only by the flap of the sail against the mast brooded over the sea. The crew slept on the seats, wrapped in their blankets, except for the helmsman, who steered his course by the Southern Cross. To glide thus through the night between the infinite sea and sky, released from all earthly contacts, gave a feeling of supernatural remoteness.

A strong wind sprang up at dawn and forced us to haul down the sail and take to our oars. The long-suffering boys had to pull until late in the afternoon, when we crossed the reef of

Monrovia and coasting along beside Cape Mesurado entered the harbor of the capital.

The view of Monrovia from the sea with its little white houses scattered like white flowers in a meadow over the gentle slopes of the Mesurado foothills was very picturesque, but disillusionment followed. The harbor lies at the mouth of St. Paul's River, and the scene as soon as we landed was one of backwardness and poverty. Noise and confusion were unceasing on the "waterside," as it is called, and the customhouse sheds and the factories of the European merchants were the only real buildings among a welter of Negro tin shanties. Negroes in ragged clothing were squatting, standing, or lying in front of the wide-open doors of white and black shopkeepers, whose shops were well stocked with goods of all sorts. Some of these loafers were street vendors, some were on the lookout for casual work, and some had no object in view which might have endangered their contemplative ease. European cars edged their way through the crowd, which gabbled noisily in native language or pidgin English; and lorries in the last stages of decrepitude rattled past. Half-naked children carried on their heads small trays containing kola nuts, bananas, and fish for sale; lean, famished dogs slunk about. New arrivals were besieged by an inquisitive mob and acquaintances were greeted with a tropical exuberance. Quarrels, laughter, and shouting could be heard on every side. The yellow dust churned up by passing motors was mingled with varied smells, of which rancid palm oil was the most penetrating. Iron roofs and walls radiated an oppressive heat only slightly modified by the sea breeze, and this added to the swelter and sweat and clamor of the crowd made it an uncommon relief to emerge into the upper town.

This was situated on the upper slopes of the long and narrow promontory. It was traversed by a few dead-straight and very wide roads, which, though paved, were covered—at least at that time—with a fine crop of grass. The center of this recti-linear layout was occupied by houses, large and small, of many styles and methods of construction, ranging from the American colonial style, including the European house at the end of the last century, beautified with columns, and down to tin huts nailed together out of old sheets of corrugated iron. But on the edges of the town could be seen many unfinished concrete houses, which the owners or contractors had not had the re-sources to complete. Broad streets ended abruptly where rocks waited to be blasted, and next door to built-up and well-tended plots there was the untamed bush, threaded by narrow tracks. Churches, stores, and government buildings in a variety of styles and sizes dominated this gay and diversified scene.

Anyone from Europe who saw the town for the first time might smile at the attempt to transplant a piece of America to Africa with insufficient means.

The inhabitants were quite in keeping with the architecture. The forefathers of most of them, a generation or two back, were slaves in the southern states of America, poor devils who dreamed of being owners and masters, which to them was the best that life could possibly offer. And now here were their descendants swaggering about proudly as the bosses of the country, in clothes as smart as the façades of their European-style houses, and smothered in jewels. They thought they could outdo the admired and envied white man by imitating him in externals; they did not see how unsuited their clothes were to the climate or realize that racial and social prejudice were as ridiculous in their case as in others.

There were those too who, having less wealth at their dis-posal, felt they must at all costs give proof in other ways of the highest culture. The aim of showing just how civilized they were inspired everything they did. Even poor natives who had only lived for a short time in these surroundings, although they could not lay claim to wealth, could at least claim to be anything rather than "bush niggers." Instead of respecting the centuries-old experience of their forefathers in their styles of building and dress, they had to adopt the pitiful tin shanty, the plate glass spectacles, and the secondhand tweed suit to show that they were not niggers, but colored gentlemen. They made a farce of superiority and turned politics into intrigue and business into a swindle. Even a sound tooth had to have its skullcap of gold foil.

And yet, laugh at them as one must sometimes, it was impossible not to like them for their many good qualities, above all for their generous hospitality. Love of laughter, a sense of humor, deep religious faith, good nature, and love of peace form the basis of their character. They are often reproached for their liking for litigation, but it only arises from a desire to show up and talk from a love of gambling for high stakes. Certainly it has no connection with pugnacity, malice, or envy.

The diplomats, missionaries, doctors, and business men who lived in this black capital city were not numerous. They had a social life of their own in the European club. Nearly every nation was represented, and among the elder men particularly there were several interesting characters; fate had played them many a strange trick before bringing them at last to this "tin can" republic.

One of my evenings was spent with the three most interesting and original men in Monrovia. One was my host, the German consul general, who gave us an excellent dinner, with several bottles of old Rhine wine, on the mosquito-proof veranda of his fine house. He was a tall and heavily built man of sixty whose hair was turning gray at the temples, but the humor of his native Rhineland still twinkled in his eyes. He was a diplomat of the old school who had spent half a lifetime in important posts under the various governors of German and British Colonial Africa. He took a detached view of the clamorous day to day problems, and I later had the impression, on many a ceremonial occasion, that an ironical or sarcastic comment was on the tip of his tongue instead of the conventional phrases.

Opposite him in a big armchair sat Bishop Campbell, of the American Episcopal Church, in a white monk's cowl, wearing a large gold pectoral cross; a broad purple sash surrounded his ample waist. His head was covered with curly red hair, as befitted a trueborn Irishman. He had merry and lively blue eyes and bushy red eyebrows, and his full red cheeks were edged by a short red beard. He was a monk of the same order as my Fathers at Bolahun and since being enthroned as a bishop at the age of fifty had held the see of Monrovia. Wild as his hair was, you could not miss his profound goodness and integrity.

The third of this select trio of elderly men with whom I spent the evening was Dr. Fuszeck, Minister of Health. He was a Hungarian, and even today his heart beat faster as he recalled how, as a Honved lieutenant, he had strewn the pavement outside the house of his beloved with dark red roses when he called to take her to the Corso. Thirty years in Africa had not affected his elegant way of life, but good living had increased his girth and he waged daily warfare with his corpulence. As the one white member of a black cabinet he was at the hub of the political life of Liberia, knew all its intrigues, and played his part with extreme adroitness and outstanding success. In addition he was an experienced and talented doctor and a lively and delightful companion.

He introduced me next morning to the President of Liberia, Edwin Barkley, who thanked me in very kind terms for my campaign against smallpox in the interior. He was a short, pock-marked Negro of middle age. He wore a black suit and was sitting informally at his large desk, smoking a pipe. In contrast with the surroundings of his high office he was entirely natural and easy. I got the impression that he was less afflicted than his officials and Ministers with an inveterate distrust of the white man, or else he knew how to conceal it. Perhaps he was in a particularly good mood because he had just successfully resisted an interference by the neighboring French and British Colonies through the League of Nations, and in this, as the interference was concerned with sanitation, he had found the help of European doctors very valuable.

So the audience went off very smoothly, and after I had drunk a glass of presidential port we rejoined Dr. Fuszeck and had a semi-professional discussion with Mr. Cooper, the Minister for the Interior.

On the previous evening at the German Consulate we had had a stimulating talk about the relations between whites and blacks, and now I was eager to hear the views of an intelligent Negro on this question. The loquacious Minister for the Interior needed no prompting to embark on a lengthy and heated discourse.

It was not true, he maintained, that the white races had any mental superiority over the black, which entitled them to assume the leadership. The Republic of Liberia itself was a living contradiction of the idea. Yet they stood alone, while all the rest of Africa was held in bondage by Europe. A single star was seen shining in their flag. It was the mustard seed sown by God, of which a tall tree would grow, overspreading the whole black continent. They no longer needed the whites, who in any case pursued only their own selfish aims. If the whites wanted to do anything for them, let them put their capital and knowledge at the blacks' disposal. Or, if they did not wish to impart their knowledge, they should at least leave the blacks free to acquire it. Mr. Cooper acknowledged the contribution made by white people to his country, but that did not make up for the closed doors the Negro came up against elsewhere in the world. The best thing would be for the whites to keep right out and leave the blacks to develop in their own way.

Most of the civilized Negroes in Liberia with whom I later discussed the matter were equally outspoken. "Money and knowledge mean power," and that was the goal they strove for. They felt no gratitude to Europeans for any help in this respect, only resentment that much had been withheld, in their view unjustly.

Though it may be different in other parts of the continent, yet when the dominion of the white man comes to an end in Africa, as it has in Asia, gratitude to the white man, who has brought them so far, will be no more than sporadic and without any significant influence on the radical attitude of black to white. Far louder and more significant will be the voices of those who declaim with reason against the injustice and brutality of the white man while he was still lord and master. For after all, taking the bad with the good, we must ourselves admit if we are honest, that we have thought far too much of our own immediate profit and of the present and too little of the black man's soul and of the future.

Can a man bring happiness and peace to others who cannot maintain either in his own house. . . ?

One day my ship put in and took me and the astounded

Massa and the shivering chimpanzee, Puck, to Germany. It was a cold and stormy voyage.

Happy and contented as I had been in Africa and determined as I was to return there, the first houses of Cuxhaven on the snowy plain, against the red sunset of a cold and misty December afternoon, were a heart-stirring sight. There once more was dear old Germany, to which I was bound by such strong ties and which I could never forget, however long my absence. It was still my native land, and the weeks and months I spent on leave there owed half their joy to this fact.

Exciting days followed, Christmas, New Year, and Shrovetide carnival; and my two African followers, Massa and Puck, joined in it all. Puck had a place made for him in the cellar where the furnace was, and there he could safely play about as he liked until an official of the Berlin Zoo came for him. But before that there was one exciting episode.

One evening, when the snow was falling in large flakes and the whole family was at dinner, heart-rending cries were suddenly heard from the street. We jumped up in alarm and hurried out armed with sticks. There was no one to be seen but an old woman who delivered newspapers, standing on the footpath outside our neighbor's house, screaming for help. Under her long wide skirts, clinging round her legs, and likewise crying out with all his might, was Puck, who had escaped by the cellar window, and then in mortal terror and freezing with cold had taken shelter with old Frau Schutz. He was delighted to jump into Massa's arms and was carried straight indoors. It took me much longer to pacify the old Mecklenburg newspaper woman, who had never seen a chimpanzee in her life, let alone harbored one under her skirt suddenly in the dead of night. She was sure at first that she had seen the devil in person, and when Massa loomed up through the snow it only confirmed her worst fears, which were not overcome until "proper people" appeared on the scene.

As for Massa, he soon made friends. He earned money at a barber's, where I had sent him to improve his haircutting, from which I had suffered long enough. His broken German and bad jokes delighted all the youth of the town and I had difficulty in getting him out of the barber's clutches.

He posed for a sculptor too, and when he came back for the first time with the money he had earned he broke out like a true philosopher: "Doctor, this money the man has given me. What for? I have not worked, only stood. He worked. Why give me the money?"

He was often sent on errands to the inn and found everyone there almost too eager to stand him a drink. But he hit on a simple way out. He accepted each offer with thanks and turned at once to the barman: "Write down in the book—this man pays a beer for me." Then when occasion offered he went back and diminished his credit by a pint or two.

He was soon a general favorite, and could well have looked after himself on his own for good, if the time to prepare for my return to Africa had not been drawing near.

The prospect, however, was unexpectedly and suddenly altered by the financial crisis which America went through in the spring of 1933. The mission was unable to carry out its agreement. Medical activities in Bolahun had to be curtailed. The news of this reached us just as we were booking our passages in Hamburg. All arrangements had now to be canceled, and a solution was arrived at only after lengthy correspondence. Instead of returning to Bolahun I was to go to Cape Mount to take charge of the hospital there, and Krueger was to carry on for the time being at Bolahun. But Jutta had to remain in Germany.

When this delay was over I returned to Africa, accompanied for the first time by my wife. Massa, of course, went too.

After a speedy but stormy voyage we disembarked once more at Freetown, as I wanted to say good-by to Bolahun before taking up my new job at Cape Mount, and also because my household and belongings had to be seen to.

The pleasure of seeing Bolahun again was overshadowed by the prospect of leaving it for good. The highlight was a farewell voyage on the Kaiha, with my wife this time making a third. The river behaved with true courtesy and so this final forest trip was an altogether delightful episode.

Then, a month behind time, we reached our new home, which the American missionaries Dickerson and Simmonds had gotten ready for us in fine style.

We were given one of the mission houses halfway up the side of Cape Mount. It was not a very conveniently built house, but this was made up for by the wonderful view of the town, lagoon, sea, and forest. We were soon installed, and I was able to resume my work as white medicine man in a new place and in new conditions.

CHAPTER 8

Fresh Scenes

MY FIRST visit to Cape Mount had already told me that in comparison with Bolahun the situation, medically speaking, was poor. For one thing, the natives of those parts, the Vais, a very conservative and racially proud tribe, had after their unfortunate experience of the white man, reaching back for hundreds of years, lost their original childlike faith in the integrity of his intentions, a faith still alive among the natives round Bolahun; for another, my predecessors had not, perhaps, been very well suited to their task. Anyway, it meant that the work of the Cape Mount hospital could easily be done in a half day, a shocking state of affairs, to which I was not at all accustomed.

St. Timothy's Hospital as a building made a very fine impression; it was constructed of squared stone in the best style. Nevertheless, even the outside showed that it had originally been only a ward in the charge of a single nurse. One doctor had added a wing, another had made alterations to it, and a third had finally tacked on a new one. The result of these alterations and additions was what you might expect—an unsuitable and unattractive building. One wing was the sister's quarters and the other accommodated twelve sickbeds. The rest of the building provided a consulting room, a small operating theater, and a laboratory. It might be called a well-equipped cottage-hospital.

Cape Mount also came off very badly in the matter of patients when compared with the pressure of work I had experienced at Bolahun. The iron hospital beds of European pattern and their white sheets, the clean wax-polished floors, and all the usual hospital furniture were no consolation, for the beds were empty. No troops of sick Negroes crowded the clean floors, and the beautiful furnishings were no better than ornaments on a shelf. Running water and good lighting, which matter more than anything in a hospital, were lacking.

The staff consisted of a Negro sister, trained in America, and two young Negro girls, all in striped uniforms with stiffly starched white aprons, who welcomed me with much embarrassment. I would have given them all in exchange for "house surgeon" Njuma, the Empty Matchbox, or the Cock.

What should I ever make of these three helpers? How should I ever find scope for my energies in such a limited field as this?

I could not believe that the thin veneer of civilization had been so effective that there were scarcely any sick left in the district. I had seen on my journey through it that the natives in these parts were much the same as in the districts where I had hitherto been working. The explanation, therefore, could only be that the hospital conformed too much to the white man's standard, and so had lost, or had never made, contact with the natives.

The only way, in my opinion, of reviving this lifeless institution was by putting it into touch with the black world around it, so that the mutual estrangement might be overcome. Above all, the sick who came must be rapidly cured. The hospital must not be burdened with a 50 per cent operation death rate, and, lastly, the high charges for treatment must be reduced.

My fear that it would take a considerable time to get into touch with the Vai Negroes was unjustified. The reputation I had acquired at Bolahun overtook me before I knew, and owing to the distance from its place of origin it grew promptly to an inordinate size, so that the number of patients rose remarkably within a few days of my taking over. The first comers were, of course, those obdurate cases which always greet a doctor when he first arrives anywhere, those who have for years sought help in all directions, and in vain. Long sufferers from rheumatism, the deaf, victims of inoperable ulcers, or gigantic inguinal ruptures, or years-old leg ulcers and almost despairing cases of urethral stricture encamped every morning with invincible obstinacy on my veranda and tipped the scales heavily against my cherished design of effecting rapid cures.

But when I operated successfully on a leg-ulcer of nearly twenty years' standing, a very large hernia, and a case of stricture the first step towards winning confidence was made. Slowly but surely the natives overcame their reserve.

After this I had my first patients from more distant places, and when they took the news back to their villages others set out. Soon the bench on the veranda was too short, beds were all full, the staff could not get through the work, and medical stores ran out. The more the black sister tore her hair and the more the hospital was run on the rocks the greater was my joy.

The day was over for useless furnishings, for polished floors, and half a day's work was not half long enough for the doctor. The time had come to build, to lay in more stores, and to engage more staff. Sleeping Beauty had woken up.

The staff problem was the easiest to solve, as my orderlies of Bolahun came to join me as fast as Dr. Krueger could spare them. They were used to the old tempo and did their best, without my prompting, to gear up their feminine colleagues to the required speed. Nor were medical requisites and equipment hard to procure. But to provide more beds was, owing to lack of space, a very tough proposition; so was the problem of adopting the unpractical layout of the available rooms to the ever-increasing demands made upon them.

The only solution was to move the sister out of her private quarters and to build a new house for her. This nearly doubled the number of beds. We were enabled also to have a larger room as operating theater and to remove the outpatients' department from the central block.

I did not feel justified in making more extensive alterations, because I was convinced that sooner or later an entirely new hospital would have to be built.

My reputation as a white medicine man was unfortunately not all that followed me from Bolahun. Smallpox too, which had so hampered my work there, found me out again. Again I had to defer all plans and to turn the hospital into an isolation hospital. This time, of course, I had learned from experience, and I had the lymph at hand.

My difficulties now were of another kind. The civilized Liberians of American origin who lived in the place had no wish to be vaccinated, and so, when the arrival of an English boat on its way to Monrovia was notified, many of them planned to escape from my furious crusade. The Minister of Health, Dr. Fuszeck, had asked me to do my utmost to prevent the infection's spreading to the capital; and if large numbers of the black population of Cape Mount reached Monrovia by sea all my precautions would be in vain. I therefore implored the Mayor to put the port in quarantine. He consented at last, but only on condition that I accepted full personal responsibility for such a preposterous and unheard-of proceeding.

When the English steamer anchored outside the reef all fugitives desiring to board her as passengers were referred to the customhouse; here they were told that although cargo could be discharged and taken on no passengers could be allowed on board owing to quarantine. Also the customhouse boat which went out to the ship had to fly the yellow quarantine flag at her bow. Now there is nothing a true seaman dreads more than the quarantine flag, above all in these unpopular West African ports. It means nothing but unpleasantness for the whole ship's company, besides delay in reaching home. That was unquestionably what the English captain thought when he saw that the customhouse cutter was flying the yellow jack. He raised anchor and steamed off before it got within a hundred yards. Through my telescope I observed this surprising maneuver from my house and I smiled complacently. But I soon laughed on the other side of my face.

I was, of course, expecting that the thwarted passengers would complain of me to the Mayor. What I was not expecting was that a Dutch firm which had goods to ship by this steamer would make me responsible both for the delay in fulfilling their contract by the specified date and for the loss and damage which would result from having to warehouse their goods for an indefinite period. The Mayor reminded me that I had accepted full responsibility, and so I was presented by the Dutchmen with a bill for £1000. To get out of the fix I was in, I decided to ask the Government to give legal effect retrospectively to my private quarantine, since its sole purpose was the protection of the capital.

The Government, however, chose another way out of the difficulty. They appointed me Medical Officer of Health with effect from a month before. In this way the quarantine automatically became official, and the claim for damages now had no reference to me personally. The Dutchmen gave up the fight at once, and as conqueror I made what amends I could by inviting them to a good dinner.

The epidemic slowly died down; the hospital which had

been occupied even to the cellar with smallpox cases, was set free for general purposes, and the measures taken to prevent the infection from spreading to Monrovia were successful.

My new dignity as Medical Officer of Health made me responsible for the port, where as the amount of shipping was small, the duties were not very onerous, and also for public hygiene. But two hundred dollars a month was all the Government could afford for the sanitary salvation of a district the size of Mecklenburg. Out of this I had first of all to pay a sanitary inspector, who undertook on my behalf those sanitary measures so beloved of the black population. With the money at my disposal I could do very little about the malaria mosquito. The forest swamps and lagoons of brackish water were too vast. It was another matter with the dreaded yellow fever mosquito. Even though at the moment there was no immediate peril, Liberia had had a severe epidemic of yellow fever in 1929, and the great prevalence of the mosquito which was the carrier of the infection made it possible that there might at any time be another. So I turned my attention first to averting this danger, which it was not beyond our strength to do.

Having once unleashed a campaign of cleanliness, I thought it as well to tackle the plague of flies. Flies, which laid their eggs in every sort of refuse, could by greater cleanliness be deprived of their hatching places and so cease to be in such appalling numbers the carriers of all sorts of intestinal diseases, in particular the very prevalent dysentery.

Now it was the custom at Cape Mount for all owners of cows to let their beasts roam about in freedom. Just as in India, there were cows standing about or lying down everywhere, and they were a real danger, not only on account of their long and bellicose horns and unamiable tempers, but because of their close friendship with innumerable flies.

171

As the old Mayor himself was the owner of many of these cows, I had to employ all the wiles of diplomacy before I at last got him to sign an order that all cattle must be removed from the town within a month. If they had not vanished by the appointed day the owners thereof were to reckon on their being shot by order of the Government. Derisive laughter was all the reception this regulation had, and no one thought of removing even a single beast. Shortly before the time ran out I gave one more brief warning, and when there was still no response I armed my sanitary inspector, Kandekai, with my elephant rifle and ordered him to shoot one cow and one calf daily from the appointed day onward. Then I went to the hospital, in considerable suspense as to what would ensue.

After a short interval I heard three shots. So the first executions had taken place. But instead of my inspector, whom I was expecting with his report, the fat old Mayor himself appeared, puffing and blowing in his feverish excitement. He had not lost a moment; his collar was undone and his braces streamed behind him. At first he could not get a word out, and I was afraid Kandekai had at least wounded somebody, if not shot him dead. In reply to this he panted, "Worse, far worse, doctor! He has shot two of my cows and a calf!"

Good, was my first thought; but instead of uttering it I did my best to pacify him.

"But, my dear Mayor, the order was signed by yourself. It was your own desire! He only obeyed your order. What have you done with him?"

"But why mine, in heaven's name?" he replied. "And my best animals at that? He's in the lockup, if you want to know."

He refused to be pacified. But at last he had to consent to the release of the justified sinner. In case he might do Kandekai some further injury I accompanied him to the lockup.

On the way there I saw a scene of sheer comedy. The natives were chasing their cows, and the cows were running in all directions. But some had their beasts on a rope, and as soon as they saw me coming they dragged them into the water, where they stood up to their necks, each with a cow's silly face beside him, and shouted, "This isn't Cape Mount. Don't you start shooting here!"

When at last I had calmed their excitement and convinced them that the shooting was over for that day, they consented to return to dry land.

Kandekai came out of the prison, swollen with pride at having done his duty, and the Mayor in utter dismay slunk into his house. He never again signed an edict of mine, and he died six months later, from rage with the doctor and grief for his dead cows, so scandal said.

But my task was now easier. My hygienic instructions were scrupulously carried out, and when soon afterwards I turned my guns on the many stray and mangy dogs the whole population joined in with enthusiasm.

It really seemed that they began to understand what I was after, and when I tackled the drinking water and the latrines there was less and less opposition. In fact, they even came to me with suggestions of their own.

I encountered unexpected opposition, however, on one point, and it took me a long time before I got my way.

According to native custom, the dead were buried in quite shallow graves. A grave was seldom more than three feet deep. And whether they were near the shore or on the slope of the hill, the graves were frequently uncovered either by a high tide or a heavy fall of rain. Then a fearful stench of decay would pervade the whole town, unless hyenas, dogs, or other beasts quickly disposed of the corpses. Along the shore it was not possible, owing to the high level of the ground water, to dig the graves any deeper, and my suggestion that the burial places should be changed was violently opposed; and so, too, because of the extra labor, was my order that the graves on the hillside should be dug deeper. Months of argument followed before I had my way. After that, a superintendent of graves was appointed, who at each burial measured the depth of the grave with his rod.

By degrees something was done to influence their daily habits and to introduce public hygiene. With the money at our disposal it could not be much, but at least a beginning was made towards breaking down the lethargy which prevails in the tropics in these matters.

Meanwhile we had been improving the living conditions in our own house. We had employed a black carpenter to make furniture to our own designs, using some of the many beautiful varieties of timber available, and we had tried our own luck at cabinetmaking when the native craftsmen were not equal to the tasks we set them. For weeks we had worked together as painters and decorators. A comparison with my bachelor's home at Bolahun would have been greatly to its disadvantage.

It was a risky experiment to take my wife out to Liberia, and now the experiment was in full swing. Not that other Europeans had not done it successfully before, but all the same it was at that time considered hazardous. Unmarried Europeans, who were in a great majority, were of the opinion, as interested onlookers, that white women in Liberia, and particularly up-country, very soon became unhappy. They had no distractions and had to do without everything that had hitherto made life worth living. Although their husbands anxiously surrounded them with servants and gave up all thought of having children, their wives as a rule soon found the climate intolerable; they began to ail or else to tire of life without a care, and so returned to Europe. Consequently for most Europeans a Liberian marriage meant that the wife lived in Europe or America. Even if a woman was able to put up with the climate and the strangeness of tropical life, the prospect of having her first child drove her back home, and henceforward she lived in separation either from her husband or her child.

Liberia's earlier reputation as the "white man's grave" had given way to that of being the grave of happy marriages. This was so widely recognized that a large American rubber plantation had made it a rule that any white employee who married and wanted to take his wife upcountry with him must be dismissed.

I had had many of these ailing wives through my hands as a doctor, and I was convinced that the excessive solicitude of their husbands was the real reason why life in West Africa did not agree with them. Surrounded by servants, many of whom were extremely competent, they had nothing to do and no domestic responsibilities. Their husbands allowed them no share in their business concerns and they could not take on their own task of motherhood. No wonder it was the best wives who felt most thwarted and superfluous!

We therefore had taken the opposite course. My wife ran the house and garden and looked after our pets; she kept the accounts of the hospital and of the public hygiene fund with all its subsequent ramifications; while we were understaffed in the hospital she acted as anesthetist. But, above all, she was the mother of our children, who were not only born there, but remained there with us. She was so busy with these occupations that during all the years we were in West Africa she never had time to be sick or unhappy.

Our example was followed and proved to be such a good

one that by degrees more and more happy wives and mothers were to be met with in Liberia. Even the Firestone Rubber Plantation relaxed their strict embargo on married men, though I will not venture so far as to say that this innovation was due solely to our example.

Anyway, it was shown that European women could stand the tropical climate just as well as their husbands. It was astonishing too how the climate and the life there suited the children. As the usual children's ailments—measles, scarlet fever, and diphtheria—were rare in the tropics, and as malaria and dysentery were not difficult to guard against, they throve amazingly. It was amusing to see the little imps with their large helmets running about like perambulating mushrooms and playing football with little naked Negro boys.

We had one anxiety, to which for a long time we could find no answer—how to protect them from snakes without interfering with their liberty to run about where they liked. I had had my own unpleasant experiences with these creatures and was all the more anxious. There was no hope of ridding ourselves of them completely, because the rats, which infested all European houses of any age and were preyed upon by poisonous snakes, acted as an unfailing decoy. Other snakes preyed on field mice in the neighborhood of houses, and in the evening particularly they lay on the paths to warm themselves in the last rays of the sun.

We had a special bugbear at Cape Mount; it was a very large black snake which had its beat between the hospital and my house and was particularly dreaded because it was what the natives called a spitter snake, an African cobra. This one was reputed to harbor the spirit of one of their ancestors, and so was believed to be invulnerable.

I had never seen it myself until one midday, when tired out

176

with an exhausting morning's work in the hospital I was strolling home in the sultry heat without looking where I was going.
Suddenly I saw this six-foot monster slowly crossing the road
just in front of me; it was as thick as my arm, its head was
erect, and its undulating coils shone with a metallic sheen. I
have always prided myself on not being easily upset, but at the
sight of this monster I was incapable either of taking to my
heels or stooping for a stone. But without deigning to give me
more than a glance and without the least acceleration the horrible creature slowly vanished in the undergrowth. Although
this was the only time I ever saw it, it was seen at the same
spot year after year until at last it disappeared for good and all.

Our anxiety for the children was therefore very natural, and
we engaged a boy to accompany them wherever they went and
to guard them from snakes. An old Negress, on hearing of this,
came to me and said that if I would give her the wages this boy
would earn in three months she would tell me a secret which
would enable me to dispense with him. Being curious to know
what she would say, I gave her the money.

"*Loketa,*" she then began, "snakes are even greater cowards
than we human beings are. But, as we go barefoot and you
walk on rubber, they do not hear us and are frightened when
we take them by surprise. I have seen your children many a
day and have heard the noise they make as they run about. If
they always make such a noise they will never see a snake and
you can save the money you pay your snake-watchman!"

What she said was no more than the practical application
of what was to be read in all books on snakes and their habits.

So in future all we had to do was to see that the children's
outdoor games were as noisy as possible, which, of course, was
not very difficult. The snake-watchman was relieved of his

177

duties, and, in fact, the children never once encountered a snake the whole time they were in Africa.

Other beasts which might have been a danger to the children—such as scorpions, land crabs as big as two fists and armed with two powerful pincers, and horrible, hairy bird-catching spiders with claws nearly as thick as an arm—although they occasionally invaded our house, emerged only by night. They were rare visitors and far less dangerous than they were supposed to be.

The plentiful fauna of Africa tempted us, as it had tempted me at Bolahun, to set up a private zoo. Our big dog Hassan, a few chimpanzees, monkeys, a civet cat, a mongoose, two leopard cubs, a parrot, and some tortoises—all these consorted together in primitive innocence without ever falling out.

When Hassan lay down on his side to sleep after his dinner Susie, the chimpanzee, came along to plunder his teeth of the grains of rice adhering to them. Unfortunately Hassan, in spite of his intelligence, could never understand that when Susie had done with the teeth on one side of his mouth she wanted him to turn over on his other side. Susie tugged and pulled at him in great agitation, until at last he expressed his displeasure in a warning growl. Then Susie gave up and, with a resigned and injured grunt, laid her head on her friend's side and settled down to sleep too, while the parrot blinked down from his perch. Then if Hassan heard any unusual sound, up he jumped, letting Susie's head fall with a bump to the floor, and ran out. Susie, in a furious temper at being woken up, stood abusing the whole canine race for its treachery, but in spite of her curiosity she was too self-willed to run after him. The parrot bobbed about, screaming with excitement, and then suddenly gave my wife's shrill whistle for the dog. Hassan came hurrying back, looking for my wife, and when he couldn't find her lay down again. The chimpanzee recovered her temper and settled herself to sleep as before, and the parrot, complacently conscious of having done his duty, closed his eyes and dozed. Domestic peace was restored.

And yet, in spite of their friendship, Hassan was the cause of little Susie's death. All the dishes stood in a row, but each of the animals knew his own. Cats and dogs never made a mistake. The monkeys alone were rather inclined to pinch a morsel here and there, not much—just a trifle, for they well knew which were their own dishes. But on one occasion the big dog caught Susie in the act of sampling his dish. He picked her up gently by the head and put her down again two or three feet away. If she had not screamed so outrageously and struggled in Hassan's cautious grip, no harm would have come to her. As it was, the point of one of his teeth broke the skin of her forehead. The wound festered and would not heal, and finally led to her death.

This was the only accident which marred the perfect harmony in which our pets lived together. The children, needless to say, delighted in this paradise, and if my son were to ask me about his earliest playmates I should have to tell him that he shared his play pen with leopards and chimpanzees. Leopards are not as a rule the easiest of companions, but even they seemed to understand that children were often rude and clumsy and not to be held accountable. When our two cubs were full-grown animals, standing two feet high and living for safety's sake in a cage, they used to spit and snarl if I went anywhere near them; but they showed no sign of ill temper when the children went right up to the bars.

My wife could enter their cage without fear, and once when she was feeding them a puff of wind blew the door open and one of them sprang out. He raced down the hill in wild leaps to where some natives were building a garden wall. In their terror they jumped as one man over the wall. With a bound the leopard was over after them. With one accord ten trembling Negroes landed back on this side of the wall again. The leopard turned round and jumped back too. This time half the boys jumped, but half fled away screaming. I could not imagine one of our leopards really attacking a native, and so I enjoyed the full comedy of the sight. And my wife, who knew that the leopard was provoked only by all the running and scampering, called out to the Negroes to stand still, saying that the animal would then leave them alone. For a moment they stood and gaped as though my wife were out of her mind, and then they dashed away in all directions shouting, "Stand still? Not on your life!" The leopard chased one of them, who fell flat from terror just before he was overtaken, expecting every moment to feel the teeth snap to on the nape of his neck. Instead the animal merely sniffed at his legs before turning away and trotting quietly up to my wife. All the other boys had sought safety up trees and in houses, and the prostrate one did not dare to get up. We now hoped that my wife would easily capture the fugitive. But he skillfully eluded every attempt, so we had to decoy him on to the veranda and then envelop him suddenly in a large rug. Before he could get free of it we caught hold by the four corners, carried him back into his cage, and shut the door.

Our animals gave occasion for many other exciting rescues. Once a civet cat climbed out on to a casement window that was open at right angles. It was impossible to catch hold of the animal in that position and as it might have fallen twenty feet onto stones when we closed the window, it had to be caught in an outstretched blanket. Another time our large chimpanzee, Susie II, climbed up on to the roof and then apparently lost her nerve at the sight of the large expanse that fell steeply away on both sides and simmered in the sun. She did not dare make the descent, but sat on the ridge, howling dismally. When some native boys climbed onto the roof to bring her down she fled in her agitation to the far end, where none of them would venture to catch her in case he fell off. A solution was eventually found by enticing her to the middle of the ridge-coping and then flinging a tennis net over her. A number of Negroes held on to it, and when the agitated chimp was well entangled she was hauled down.

The most delightful, ingratiating, and even insinuating members of our zoo were the mongooses, little brown animals which at first sight resemble squirrels without tails. They are extraordinarily quick to take a liking to their masters. I once bought one from a native and brought it home in my trouser pocket. It sat there all the way with its head out, and for ever after its one longing was to get back. At night when we sat reading it suddenly came waddling up, jumped on to my chair, and instantly vanished into my trousers pocket. If I threw it out it was back next moment, until I finally had to give way. It was even more tiresome when it got the habit of burrowing up my right trousers leg and making itself cosy there. Sometimes it followed us into bed. It was always fastidiously clean, and it was allowed to enjoy these peculiar privileges because it was the deadliest enemy of snakes. Every snake it saw it bit to death. I had never quite been able to believe that these defenseless little creatures, for which a snake's bite would mean certain death, actually dared to do battle with a snake. But one day I had the chance of watching one of these perilous duels.

A greenish-gray snake three feet or more in length, was challenged by our mongoose in front of the house. The snake had its head erect in the manner of a cobra and kept its eyes fixed on its tiny foe, who was jumping to and fro in short, quick jumps. These amazingly quick jumps, now to this side, now to that, cheated every lunge the snake made, but it needed only one false move on its enemy's part in order to drive home its poisonous fangs. The longer the duel went on the more uncertain the snake became. The little bobbing thing seemed to irritate it, and after a number of its lunges had missed it began to strike half-heartedly; in fact, it would gladly have broken off the engagement. Suddenly the mongoose made a dart far too swift for me to follow with my eye; he had seen the right moment and seized it, and now the snake and mongoose were one whirl of dust. "He's got her, he's got her!" Massa shouted, and he could hardly be stopped from joining in the scrimmage. Soon the little hero was on his feet again, dragging the defeated foe along by the nape of the neck. He bit again and again until the snake writhed no more. Suddenly he let go and leaped back again, playing with the dead snake like a cat with a mouse.

I could go on telling stories about our pets. There was the baby chimpanzee, Orje, whom our daughter took out in her pram instead of a doll; there were the little armored creatures, related to the armadillo, which were always digging their way out of their cages; there was the young crocodile, the great crested eagle, the iguana, and the tiresome night apes. They were all a constant source of pleasure and amusement. Most came to us in infancy and would have been helpless if set at liberty. They would soon have fallen a prey to their enemies, and so when we went on leave we took them with us, and perhaps many are alive to this day in various German zoos.

Our forest solitude was enlivened also by the great number of visitors we had. As there were no hotels, every white traveler turned to his fellows, and so the hospitality prevailing among the natives prevailed also among the whites, as it used to do in ancient times. Strangers turned up and stayed a few days, and then went on their way. Some stayed on for weeks as paying guests. We were very seldom without visitors during the years we spent at Cape Mount.

One of our earliest visitors was Krueger. He came to us for the first Christmas, which otherwise he would have had to spend alone at Bolahun, and we enjoyed some very happy days together at Cape Mount. None of us could have imagined then what a hard fate lay ahead of him. He had scarcely returned to Bolahun in the highest spirits when the monks had to break the news of a sudden drop in their finances which they feared would make it impossible to maintain the hospital even in its present modest scope. But Krueger was not so easily beaten. He said he would carry on without a salary at his own risk, even though the profit to be made had hitherto been merely supplementary. He hoped to win through by hard work and strict economy. It was like him never to have asked me for help. He did not even mention his predicament, but fought his own battle alone in the forest with unflinching tenacity. Yet he broke down at last and had to return to Germany in failing health.

It was too late now for me to do anything, and I could only regret that fate had been too strong for one who had so courageously defied it. Years passed before we met again. War had broken out, and Krueger was on the point of taking up his first post as naval surgeon on board a large battleship. He was delighted to have been passed fit once more, and Jutta Kolbe, whom he had married, was now the proud and happy mother of four fine children. But once again his luck was out. His ship was the *Bismarck,* and on her this brave man met his end.

We had been more fortunate at Cape Mount. When we

returned from our first European leave we moved into a better, stone-built house, which gave room for our growing family and also for visitors.

As our own private life gradually improved, so the hospital progressed also. An American sister was engaged, and a Negro staff was trained in sufficient numbers to cope with the constantly increasing demands. The once sleepy hospital was now as lively as the one at Bolahun. The sick came from all parts, even from Monrovia, and some made the pilgrimage from the neighboring British colony of Sierra Leone.

One day I had a request from Dr. Fuszeck, the Minister of Health, to take his place in the capital for three months. I could hardly refuse, especially as I had been obliged at that very time to defer my own leave. My wife had suddenly fallen a victim to severe blood poisoning and had only been saved by the sulfonamides which had just reached me as medical samples.

I had intended traveling to Europe with the whole family as soon as my wife was past the worst and the voyage could be contemplated, but that turned out to be just the moment when, owing to the heavy seas on the reef, Cape Mount was cut off from traffic by sea. All ships had to pass by without taking off either passengers or cargo. So I had no choice but to make for Monrovia overland. There my whole family would be able to get a boat for Europe, while I perforce stayed behind to represent the Minister of Health.

The rains were just at their peak. Every day the rain came down in torrents and the rivers were all in flood. My wife still had her leg in plaster and could not stand up. Moreover, the children were still quite small. As there was every prospect that the trek would put all previous ones in the shade, we made up our minds to be undismayed by whatever might occur.

On the first day we had to be rowed the entire length of Lake Pizo because the road along the shore went for miles through what was now one great morass. Long before the end of the six-hour crossing, the roof we had erected over our seats was soaked through by the terrific weight of water falling upon it, and our waterproof sheets and cloaks were in the same state. Waterfalls poured down from the umbrellas, and a millstream ran down inside my wife's plaster bandage. Our cigarettes wilted, the loaves turned to paste, the children whimpered—it did not take more than an hour or two to take all the joy out of our trip.

So when we landed on the other side we thought it best to camp for the night at once in order to dry our things and to make better preparations for the second day in view of our experiences of the first. The next morning we set off again in the usual rain. First went four porters with the large cabin trunk, then porters in single file with the smaller cases and the provision chest. Then followed my wife in a roofed-in hammock with our three-year-old boy on her lap. Next came the "ark" with our five-months-old daughter. To ensure her comfort I had put her pram inside a cage of mosquito netting, and crowned it with a roof of corrugated iron and asbestos tiles with wide eaves to keep out the sun, as she was too young for a sun helmet. The pram itself rested on a long plank to which it was securely fastened, and the two ends reposed on two woolly heads. Thus the little princess rocked on her way high above all obstacles, squeezing her nose flat against the netting. A hospital nurse followed with dry napkins and warm milk, and I brought up the rear with the big dog Hassan.

The first great obstacle we had to negotiate was the Loofa river, over a hundred yards wide. The ferrymen had a canoe which was large enough, but was so damaged in the bows that it had to be loaded with great care in case it shipped water. I had therefore to escort my wife and children and finally the dog across one by one. In all I made seven trips before our flock was safely over. Then the baggage was ferried across.

A far more perilous crossing, however, awaited us on the following morning, and even today I shudder when I think of it.

We came to a narrow gorge about ten or twelve yards wide; the steep sides enclosed a torrent which raged along in its rocky bed fifteen feet or so below. In the dry season you could wade across it, but now it had risen five feet and was flowing so fast that the strongest man could scarcely have got across it. The natives had bridged it with a fair-sized tree trunk, and they were sure-footed enough to cross the foaming torrent without feeling giddy. The trunk had been stripped of its bark and the rain had made it as smooth as glass. The little shallow notches our boys cut in it did not diminish its slipperiness in the slightest degree. However, cross it we must or go back the whole way we had come. The porters with the tin trunks had made nothing of it, and now the heavy cabin trunk followed, swinging on a long pole between two strong porters.

Next we entrusted our small son, telling him to keep as still as a mouse, to a reliable boy and hoped for the best. They were scarcely halfway across—our son keeping admirably quiet all the time—when to our horror we saw that the two porters who held the pram swaying on their heads had followed on without a moment's delay, and without even waiting to be told. We had intended to take the little girl out of the pram and give her to Flumo, the reliable porter who was carrying our son across. Instead she was precariously swinging across in the ark! We did not dare call them back; we hardly dared breathe until our little darlings were safely on the other side.

Flumo came back laughing. "There, Missis, and now it's you." He was not very powerfully built, but he made little of taking my wife on his back in spite of the heavy plaster on her leg. He took a few steps to get his load adjusted and then carried it without wavering to the other side.

Now it was Hassan's turn, but nothing would induce him to venture on the slippery trunk, nor in his agitation at being parted from his mistress would he allow anyone to get hold of him. I saw that I should have to take him through the water. I could not let him go alone. He would never have kept his footing on the smooth round boulders and once in would have been carried away. I undressed and, catching him by the collar, plunged into the stream. After many tumbles and scrambles we too got safely across.

Since those days we have often wondered whether we would go through all our African adventures a second time. We agree that we should not like to cross that gorge again, even though it all passed off so well.

The rest of the journey was simple; even the rain had the decency to leave off. The sun shone, and we reached the capital in fairly good trim. My family embarked for Europe in the next boat of the Woermann Line and I remained behind to perform the duties of Health Minister.

The budget of the highest authority for health was, like my own as a local Medical Officer, very small, but the duties made a change from those of a white medicine man in the forest. The black President and the other black excellencies were now my patients instead of chiefs and bush-Negroes. The ailments were correspondingly different. I now dealt with migraines, neuroses, overwork, and other diseases of civilization instead of diarrhea, elephantiasis, and ulcers. Instead of snapping fingers with chiefs in a palaver house, I now danced a *polonaise* at the

187

ball in celebration of the Independence Day of the Republic with Her black Excellency, the wife of the Minister for the Interior, and conversed about Chopin and Tschaikovsky with the Minister of Finance. Indeed, the receptions and parties of white and black notabilities were more fatiguing than a day's hunting in the bush.

At last Dr. Fuszeck returned and I could go on leave.

It was of great interest to get to know the leading men of the black republic and to have a glimpse of its diplomatic affairs. But I felt no desire to stay in Monrovia and take over the Government hospital, as I was invited to do.

After a wonderful leave in Europe I was glad to return to my forest home with my wife, now quite well again, and my children and my dog, there to work on at the building up of my own little kingdom.

CHAPTER 9

Leopards and Leopard-men

AT CAPE MOUNT, as at Bolahun, leprosy, one of the oldest diseases of mankind, was a great distress to me. At that time it was scarcely possible to cure it, and the terrible martyrdom and misery in which the lives of sufferers from it ebbed away was all the more distressing to see.

The natives are well aware of the symptoms, course, and nature of the disease, which had scourged them for thousands of years. They knew that there was no cure for it and that even after many years it seldom caused death, but almost always led to horrible deformities and mutilations, with the loss of whole limbs, incurable ulcers of great size, and sometimes even blindness, until at last some other illness supervened to release the human wreck from a life of hunger and destitution.

It is hardly surprising then that they feared the *"na szianga"* ("red sickness") more than all others. They avoided the victim of it and all association with him for fear of getting within the magic circuit which had gained such dread power over him. As long as the leper could conceal his state and had the strength to go on working he was not in need, even though the part he played in village life dwindled and his loneliness, both inward and outward, increased step by step. Gradually the day drew near when he could no longer provide for himself and his family. It was then, just when the healthy members of the community ought to have come to his help, that he became an outcast. He had to sell all his possessions bit by bit merely to

189

exist, and was finally forced to beg and steal. The villagers would have driven him out altogether had they not been afraid that the malevolent spell might then have affected them also. So the village had grudgingly to put up with his presence until death came as a merciful release for him and for it.

The victims knew that even the white doctor had no cure, but they came to him all the same. They hoped he might at least alleviate the large ulcers and mutilations, and perhaps relieve their hunger and destitution for the time being.

At Bolahun there were between twenty and thirty lepers in palm-leaf huts near the hospital town who came to the hospital to have their sores dressed and to receive their pittance of rice and oil. They were too few in comparison with the rest of the sick to make much difference or to constitute a social problem.

It was quite another matter at Cape Mount. The humanitarianism constantly preached by the whites had had its effect, and the natives were not so ruthless as they were in the remoter depths of the forest. They allowed the lepers to associate with them and even to work with them, if they were able to, or to work at some handicraft of their own. The penalty of isolation was enforced only when the sores and deformities of the afflicted persons were too nauseating. Sometimes, of course, Liberians of American origin were affected. In their case no one thought of isolation; their families cared for them even when their affliction had reached an advanced stage. Among the lepers I came across were a teacher in a boy's school, a fisherman, and a marketwoman selling provisions.

This attitude of the civilized Negro, as well as the greater tolerance shown by the native-born Negro, was of course admirable as an expression of neighborly love, but disastrous from the point of view of preventive hygiene. The disease was invited to spread far and wide, and the number of lepers was much greater than in the remoter districts.

I could not resist the conclusion that the biological balance had been upset, since there was less leprosy among the Negroes whose way of life had been maintained undisturbed for thousands of years than among those who were undergoing the influence of civilization. It is always said that leprosy, like consumption, is a disease of poverty and destitution. But I got the impression that at least with leprosy, poverty and destitution were the results and not the original factors. In any case, the higher standard of life among the natives, owing to the first impact of civilization, clearly did nothing to arrest it. On the contrary, in so far as civilization inculcated a more sympathetic attitude and a less ruthless isolation of the sufferers, it increased the risk of contagion. Leprosy, which formerly had a subordinate place on the map of disease, now had a very large one.

It followed that something had to be done to restore the balance. In nearly all tropical countries and African colonies lepers had been cared for in some organized manner for many years past, but in Liberia my efforts to inaugurate something of the kind met with an unexpected rebuff from the Government. The country was poor; there were other more pressing problems awaiting a solution. My proposals for setting up the organization with the financial support of the international Mission to Lepers were likewise declined. The Republic of Liberia, which in those days stood in constant dread of superintendence by the League of Nations, did not wish it to become known that there was leprosy in the country and that nothing was done to control it, because this would give the League a new excuse for interference and might possibly lead to loss of independence. My humanitarian efforts were therefore a menace to high interests of state and were severely criticized and frowned upon. But by 1936 the threatening clouds of League of Nations trusteeship had retreated, and I succeeded at long last in putting my proposals through. Even so, the Government declined to assume any official responsibility for a leper colony, but it put a small sum of money at my disposal and allowed me to interest the above-mentioned philanthropic society in the lepers of Liberia.

The large-scale campaign I had planned was therefore barred; but still I was enabled to go ahead with a leper colony on lines of my own.

About five miles from Cape Mount, just where Lake Pizo has its outlet to the lagoon and the open sea, there was a flat and uninhabited island called Massateen. It measured eight or nine square miles; mangroves grew in a thick fringe along its shores, and inland there were innumerable oil palms. In the thick undergrowth of the swampy places there were great numbers of raffia palms, from the leaves of which the valuable raffia is obtained. There was excellent fishing. Springs of fresh water were available. In fact, a good number of people could be settled there in strict isolation; and though it was too far from the town and the hospital at Cape Mount for frequent intercourse, it was near enough for the necessary supervision and control.

My plan was to isolate the lepers there, but not in one of the usual leper colonies, where lepers were kept in idleness year after year and confined to the same set of buildings until they were bored and discontented. Charity is soon taken for granted, and without the incentive to work life quickly becomes tedious. There is no satisfaction like striving for what you need. That alone makes life worth living.

I resolved therefore that the people I installed on this island

192

should not receive alms or live a life of idleness. They should be given only what would enable them to earn their living and satisfy their needs. If I was right my lepers would necessarily find happiness on their island and never wish to leave it.

As it turned out, only five out of a hundred and ten deserted during the three years of the colony's existence, although no watch whatever was kept; and of those who were cured only two asked to leave. All the rest chose to stay on.

As soon as I received the first grant from the Government I took some healthy boys to the island and looked for a suitable spot for the settlement. I only had the necessary area cleared, a spring dug out, and three native huts and a house for the resident nurse built. The required stock of tools was deposited with the nurse, and then the first lepers were "planted out" on the island. If they wanted to remain there they had to work, because otherwise they could not draw their daily ration of rice, which the nurse was to give them until their first harvest.

The leper colony grew steadily of its own accord. Soon there were ten, and then twenty, houses occupied. An open palaver house was erected, and near the nurse's house there arose a small hospital, a school, and a church. Gardens were fenced, roads made, and bridges built. Hens, ducks, dogs, and goats were added to the population. Fishing prospered, and a carpenter's shop provided doors and furniture. After the first rainy season a large communal farm supplied the population with its staple article of diet, rice. In a surprisingly short time these outcasts of humanity had made my dream come true, and, above all, these poorest of the poor were happy.

They soon proved, for example, that their daily labor produced more rice than they needed, and so, after the approved Bolahun pattern, I put in money of my own and paid them for the work they did in building up the settlement. They were divided into three classes of workers, not according to their disablement, but according to the amount of work they actually did. The first class was paid about 80 per cent of the wage customary in the country. After they had earned a bare living they could go on to achieve a modest standard of comfort by their work. The nurse took charge of their money at its full value and bought them such luxuries as they desired in Cape Mount.

They could by greater exertions work their way into the higher classes, and from the highest class they could rise to being craftsmen. These craftsmen had special pay. Also they harvested their palm kernels, palm oil, and raffia, and made charming little mother-of-pearl boxes. All these I sold for them to the best advantage I could, and what I made on them was returned to the settlement.

The colony elected its own chief to rule over its internal affairs, and he was also the leader of the first-class workers. The keenest interest was taken in the development of the colony, and my own part was soon confined to the necessary supervision.

They were assiduous attendants at the school and church which the mission had erected on the island. As for their festivals, dances, and entertainments, they saw to these themselves on a liberal scale. But there were two things which especially contributed to their happiness. One was that they soon saw a real amelioration of their disease from the chaulmoogra oil treatment; in some cases all clinical symptoms vanished. These cured cases withdrew to a separate settlement on the island, where they lived in complete liberty. They gave this settlement the poetic name of New Hope.

The second source of happiness was that they were permitted to marry. Most of them were already married in their "other" life, but in only two cases had the partner come as well. I had some trouble in persuading the mission that these "immoral" marriages were necessary. But at last the missionaries agreed that they were the best solution of many problems. So now there were proper households and regular married life. Also the leper children who came to the island now found good homes waiting for them. They were distributed among the island households.

The income of a married leper in each class was a third larger than that of the unmarried, and it was raised by a further third for each adopted child, so that many men earned a higher wage than they ever could "outside."

They now had all that in their eyes stood for life: the power to earn a livelihood, a house, a wife and child, and the hope of one day being cured. Life "outside" had not as much to offer them, and so they had no desire to return to it. Here they were happy, and here they meant to stay.

My aim was achieved. The outcasts of humanity had found a basis of life again and had not, in spite of isolation, lost heart and the power to be happy. My colony also did away with the increased risk of contagion which arose when the primitive and ruthless way of dealing with the diseased was upset by the ideal of loving one's neighbor.

Of course there were difficulties with which originally I had not reckoned. And for one thing the institution of these leper marriages naturally had the usual consequence of producing offspring.

To meet this contingency, I arranged for the prospective mothers to have their babies in the isolation department of the hospital. Since leprosy is not transmitted, the children were born healthy, but of course would soon have been infected by their mothers. Mother and child were therefore parted immediately after the child was born. This may sound cruel, but I explained the necessity for it in a long talk, and the lepers understood. They would rather their children were healthy in the hands of strangers than doomed to acquire the hateful malady before their eyes. So the mother returned to the island and the child remained in the hospital.

The first was a boy, who was given the fine name of Massateen-Kai (Massateen man). I handed him over to the nurses as their common charge and took the opportunity of giving them practical instruction in the rearing of children and particularly in artificial feeding. The joy and enthusiasm of the nurses was great, and Massateen-Kai lived like a prince.

But the great number of babies became an embarrassment. We soon had fifteen living proofs of the happy marriages of the islanders. There were no orphanages or anything of the kind anywhere in the country, and I was in a fix as to what to do with these infants.

At last I let it be known that I wished to hear of foster mothers and would give them good pay. Those Negro wives who presented themselves and were found suitable were provided by a donor in America with a complete baby outfit which was so generous that it clothed their own child as well as the adopted one.

The mother had to bring the foster child to the hospital for inspection once a week. If the child was healthy and well cared for she took twenty shillings home with her at the end of the month.

At the end of six months the payment was reduced to ten shillings, and at the end of the next half year to five, and ceased altogether after a further six months. The foster mother might then return the child to us, and the great question then arose— which would she do? Would she have become so fond of the child that she would keep it as her own, or would she leave it on our hands?

My gamble on Negro mother love was a complete success. We did not have one child back. On the contrary, the foster mothers were in a panic lest we might resume possession of the children committed to their care.

I had many such problems to worry me, and on the island itself there were many touching human stories, one of which I remember well. It concerned Findah and Fodi.

Findah was a fourteen-year-old girl who had been brought to me by her parents suffering from a serious infection of the marrow of the thighbone and a contraction of both knees. As I could not take her into the hospital at once, her parents found a lodging for her with a leper named Fodi, a man in his twenties, who had previously been employed as a chauffeur in Sierra Leone and now earned his living by fishing. He was not an advanced case; he had only patches on his hands and face. Fodi was attracted by the pretty girl, although she could only creep on her hands and knees. Perhaps he thought also that as an outcast he might not find it easy to get anyone else as a wife, and so he bought her from her parents for a small sum. When the time came for Findah to be taken into the hospital, Fodi's time also had come to settle on Massateen. By slow stages Findah recovered the use of her knees, and the infection of the thigh bone was cured. As her health improved she grew into the prettiest girl of the place, and I never thought she would consent of her own free will to join Fodi on the island. But one day she came along on her crutches and asked to join her husband. She brushed aside all my well-meant warnings. She wanted to be with Fodi.

I now saw them both regularly on my weekly visits to the island, apparently contented and happy together; and I was astonished that Findah's love was so strong that she could face isolation and all the risks of becoming a leper merely to be with her sick husband.

I was all the more astonished when she suddenly appeared at my house one day with a woebegone face. Fodi had beaten her and driven her out. Sorry as I was for her in her grief and disappointment, I could not help rejoicing that her marriage with Fodi, the leper, was at an end and that she might perhaps, after all, be spared the fate of becoming a leper herself. So I abused Fodi for all I was worth, and forbade Findah ever to return to the island. She agreed, and was lodged with a trust-worthy Negro in the neighborhood until her mother could take her home.

On my next visit to the island I had a talk with Fodi. He said he was as fond of Findah as ever, but had finally decided to give her up because of his disease. I promised to see that the money he had given for her was repaid him, and he promised in return to take no steps to get her back.

I really felt I had done a good deed, and was very proud of myself when the mother arrived and I could announce my solution of the predicament. But when I sent for Findah, I was told that she had quietly taken herself off to Fodi early that morning.

And had he the strength to send her back again? Did he stand firm and keep his word? He flung himself on the ground at my feet and implored me to leave him his wife. He swore by heaven and hell that he would leave nothing undone for her if only she might stay.

It was now up to me. Could I harden my heart against such love?—I left poor Findah and Fodi, the leper, to live out their happiness and their sorrow together.

We had made a sort of depot for Massateen on a tongue of

land opposite the island and close to the village of Tosso. Particularly in the early days, a great many things—such as seed, cuttings of pineapple, banana, orange, and lemon trees, tools, medical stores, and medicines—had to be sent out, and later palm oil, raffia, and other products had to be brought in for sale on the mainland. All these things were transported in open dugouts across the half mile or more of water. New colonists were paddled across in them too, and once a week I made use of this ferry myself.

These native canoes had made the passage across the lake countless times in perfect safety. It was my luck to be on board on the only occasion when a frightful disaster occurred.

I had taken my head theater nurse across on one of my weekly visits to Massateen, as I had one or two operations to perform. Besides her, there was a native boy who wanted to visit his sick father, and a porter who was taking various things required on the island. When our work was done we set out on the return journey, with a great send-off from the landing stage. As usual, the last injunction to be shouted after us was to beware of the great crocodile, who had his headquarters on a sandbank we had to pass on our way.

"Old Uncle's not at home," our ferryman observed when we passed the sandbank without seeing our friend. "He's out with his brothers."

The voyage went smoothly enough until we were four or five hundred yards from the spit of land for which we were making. Then quite suddenly a squall struck us amidships. Little waves rose from the smooth surface and broke against our boat, which was scarcely eight inches out of the water. In vain I tried to make the ferryman see that he must paddle the boat round in a sharp turn to face the waves. Before he understood what I meant, we had shipped one wave after another and were so low in the water that we were awash. But the situation was not utterly hopeless until the ferryman suddenly lost his head completely and shouting "We're sinking, we're sinking," plunged head first into the lake. The canoe now sank in earnest, and the four of us who were left, of whom I alone could swim, got out and tried to hold on to its sides. I hoped it might still keep us afloat, but in this I was deceived. It was made of a very heavy wood and sank like a stone.

The sister and boy now clung to me in terror, but the porter endeavored to keep himself on the surface by his own efforts. I was not trained in lifesaving; all the same I thought I could bring the two safely across the short stretch of water between us and shore.

No doubt this was too much to expect; to my great grief I was very soon obliged, in order to save the nurse, to let go of the boy, who was drowned at once. I then endeavored, swimming according to the prescribed method, to reach land with the nurse. When I thought we must be near I turned my head to look and saw to my horror that in spite of all my exertions we were no nearer than when we started. I was in despair, particularly as the weight of my shoes was slowly tiring me out. If I were ever to reach land I had to get rid of them. But they had soaked themselves so tightly to my feet that it was merely a loss of time and strength to struggle with them. While doing so I twice lost hold of the nurse, and by the time I had got hold of her for the second time, I no longer had the strength to hold her up and at the same time to prevent her from grappling me. We both sank before I could get free, and when I came to the surface again in an exhausted state I was alone.

The full horror of the disaster now dawned on me. I did not understand why I was unable to reach the shore. I was seized by the dread of never reaching it at all, and almost at the same moment I remembered the crocodiles with which the lake was infested. With the energy of despair I swam towards the tongue of land, which seemed after all so near. I looked down at the bottom through the transparent water, and it told me that struggle as I might I was not gaining an inch. There was only one explanation: the current of the lake's ebb tide was diverted by the projecting spit of land, and was set dead against me. All my efforts had done no more than keep me stationary.

I now gave up and went with the current, at the same time trying by slow degrees to draw out from it; and in this I finally succeeded. With my last grasp I reached a sandbank ten or twelve yards from the shore. I stood up in the water to rest, so exhausted that I did not dare swim those last yards which parted me from the land. It was not until the villagers of Tosso, who had flocked to the shore in great excitement as soon as they knew of the disaster, warned me of the crocodiles that I recovered my energy. Not one of them had the courage to come to my help, which was not surprising.

And now, far out in the lake, carried away on the current, they saw a man swimming. They quickly launched a canoe and hurried to the rescue of the ferryman, who had kept afloat by letting himself go with the current.

All the rest were drowned. It was a bitter experience. The people streamed out in crowds from Cape Mount, rejoicing to welcome their doctor safely home again, but never was a triumphal welcome more painful.

The disaster had one good result. The Government put a motor speedboat at our disposal for our journeys to the island. This made the visits to Massateen a pleasure. Also I was able to reach places up the river and on the lake far more quickly when my services were required. But the lives of three human beings was too heavy a price to pay. And now week after week the natives insisted that I must make an offering in person to the mother of all crocodiles as thanks for my miraculous rescue. This meant a journey to Szowi, the famous place where from time immemorial the mother of all crocodiles had made her home and ruled as paramount chief. I had often heard of this prodigious beast, but had never seen her.

The natives maintained that when two men had a quarrel she was summoned and that forthwith she crawled the whole length of the village to the palaver house. Each of the two parties to the dispute then put his case in a speech of fiery eloquence, and in conclusion laid his offering, consisting of a white cock, two kola nuts, and a bottle of rum, at her side. The verdict went to him whose offering she accepted by overturning the bottle of rum. She then had the two bottles emptied down her throat, devoured the two kola nuts and lastly the cocks, and withdrew again to her native element.

The story of this rum-drinking crocodile had never seemed to me worthy of belief. I believed neither that she was over a hundred years old nor that she brought her children when they reached a certain age, together with all her descendants, into the village to be introduced to the inhabitants.

The new motorboat gave me the opportunity of getting to the bottom of this Negro fairy tale, and one day, when the omens were favorable, we set off for Szowi, which is situated on a shallow backwater of the river, running almost parallel to the shore of the lake. Our boat grounded on a marshy sandbank a good hundred yards from the little village, and although we soon got her off again, all our efforts to reach the landing place were in vain, because it was the dry season and the water was too low. Since the famous crocodile was after all a civil beast, we decided to anchor where we were and to wade the rest of the distance. It was useless to take the shortest route to the bank because of the impenetrable mangrove thickets. To be on the safe side, however, I held my rifle ready. But nothing happened, although the stretch of water was somehow rather more uncomfortable than we had supposed from the security of our boat.

We then awaited the chief in the palaver house and when he came, announced our desire to see the famous beast.

"Have you two cocks with you, a white and a black?" he asked me.

I deeply regretted that we had not. "If you have no cocks to offer the crocodile will not come and your journey is wasted."

Even when I asked him to sell me two cocks suitable for the purpose there were further difficulties.

"Ah, *loketa,* scarcely anyone has cocks in these hard times, and if they have they do not want to sell them. You will have to pay a great deal of money for them.

I was not going to be put off with that. I wanted to know for myself what was at the bottom of this tale. So I offered to pay whatever was asked on condition that I might return the birds and have my money back if the prodigy did not appear. To my astonishment the chief agreed instantly and at once the whole village turned out in a wild hunt for cocks, which ended in my being offered two lamentable specimens at ten times the current price. They were making a good thing out of their local celebrity. How glad I was I had brought a bottle of rum with me. I certainly could not have paid the local price. But that had not been in my mind. I had only wanted to make sure that the beast had genuine rum and not, perhaps, water.

The crocodile was now summoned. Two boys got into a shallow dugout, and while one paddled it around, the other beat the two unfortunate birds together, at which they naturally squawked loudly. After this short tour the two boys returned to the landing stage and walked slowly through the village to the palaver house, beating the two cocks together all the time. They had hardly left the bank when suddenly there arose from the mirror-smooth water the great head of a Nile crocodile followed by the whole of her huge armored body and long jagged tail. Like a dragon of legendary days this enormous beast, about thirteen feet in length, waddled slowly on behind the two boys. She would have been a frightening spectacle but for the astonishing sight of the Negro children standing close to her as she passed. When she reached the palaver house she stopped in the middle of the open floor, while we as well as the inhabitants sat on the low balustrade. The chief next stepped up to the crocodile and addressed her in a long speech, announcing my presence and—without any authority from me —explaining that I had come to give thanks for my rescue after the disaster of the ferryboat and to swear eternal friendship. Then he took one of the costly birds and threw it at the beast's enormous gaping jaws. At the same instant, however, the lower jaw snapped up with incredible speed. The terrified cockerel fell on the ground and was immediately covered by the creature's chin, as with the same rapidity she again opened her hideously gaping maw just as though nothing had occurred. The chief thereupon offered the bottle of rum I had brought. He went up to her with a continuous murmur of unintelligible words and slowly poured the rum from above into her open jaws. The crocodile scarcely moved her tongue, and the whole contents of the bottle disappeared without anything particular to show for it. The frightful gullet still remained obdurately open and the yellow eyes rolled their slits of pupils slowly to and fro. Obviously she was awaiting the second cock, and it was now thrown to her. This time the jaws closed on it. She then

204

quickly drew her great bulk back just far enough to expose the first cock beneath her chin. In a flash the dead bird was seized in the sawlike teeth, whereupon the crocodile turned in her own length with amazing adroitness and rapidly went back to the river, in which she vanished without a ripple or a sound.

The renowned and sacred crocodile of Szowi was therefore no myth, but although we had convinced ourselves of the beast's peaceable disposition and had even sworn eternal friendship, not one of us was eager to wade back to our motorboat. The thought that we might inadvertently tread on our new friend under water was too painful, and so we had ourselves paddled out in the shallow dugout, in spite of the wide grins occasioned by our heroic display of courage.

Probably the crocodile of Szowi was the origin of the strange idea, cherished by the Negroes of the Vai tribe, that these dangerous reptiles were well disposed towards men and therefore ought not to be hunted or killed. They clung to their belief even though from time to time a man was seized and devoured.

When such a disaster occurred the Vais excused their friends by saying that there were criminals among men too; yet it was not right to condemn all men; only the murderer himself ought to be destroyed. And so they assembled to pass judgment on the crocodile concerned and condemned it to death. Hunters were then sent out with the strict order to kill only the guilty one. When the execution had been done, and the hunters came back with the body, an autopsy was held to make sure that it was the right one. And if so, they were convinced that they had not lost the friendship of the crocodiles, but rather had earned their gratitude by executing the renegade. This gave ample excuse for holding a great feast and for according the reptiles a further lease of liberty and license.

I once chanced to see what insolent use they could make of

it. I was in a Negro's house near the edge of the lagoon. A little terrier ran along the road, which was about five yards from the shore. Suddenly one of these monsters rose out of the water and snapped up the dog before he could even think of escape.

On one occasion I was present at the autopsy held to prove whether the hunters had duly executed the criminal. A crocodile who had seized a small boy when he went to draw water had been killed the same day. It was fifteen to twenty feet long, and when it was cut open in Cape Mount market place the cap and part of one of the boy's legs were taken from the stomach. I had the head of this crocodile stuffed in memory of the inquest.

I never had occasion to deal with wounds caused by crocodiles, because they drag their victims under and drown them. I never, indeed, dealt with wounds caused by any of the larger animals excepting the bites or scratches of leopards. For a time I was concerned with these too closely for my liking.

One day a woman from a nearby village came to me in a terrible state, bringing her ten-year-old son, who had suddenly been fallen upon by a leopard in the dark on his way from one house to another. He had been seized by the thigh, but very surprisingly the animal had let go of him at once and vanished when his terrified screams brought the neighbors running from their houses. The boy was found lying on the ground with deep flesh wounds in his thigh, and at dawn indistinct tracks of a leopard were to be seen in the village.

The little boy's wounds were severe, and there was every reason to expect that as with all wounds caused by beasts of prey they would fester and prove mortal. Fortunately they healed remarkably well, and finally I was able to stitch up the badly torn muscles. Even more extraordinary than this rapid healing of a wound caused by a leopard's carrion tainted claws

was the behavior of the mother. She implored me in great
agitation to keep the boy with me always, even after he was
cured. She would never be able to pay me for what I had done,
but instead of payment I could keep the boy, to whom I had
given a second birth—that is, whose life I had saved—until she
could redeem the pledge. I had had similar offers made me
occasionally before this, but never with such urgency and such
unmistakable signs of anxiety for the child. I suspected that
some superstition or "magic" was behind it, but I could get
nothing out of her, and finally I kept the boy.

Nor did I pay much attention to the wild talk of the natives
about leopards, and how their time for human prey had come
round again with the dry season.

It was a surprise when I very soon had to look into the question more closely. The old and venerable chief of Tosso, the
little place near which I had so nearly been drowned, asked
me to give my opinion about the cause of a girl's death. Had
she been mauled by a leopard or had she died from some other
cause? I found this query rather odd, but when he told me
that some man had possibly committed the murder and
made it appear that death had been caused by the fangs of
a leopard I took the matter up with alacrity. The prospect of
holding a coroner's inquest in the forest tempted me, and I set
off for Tosso with the chief as soon as I could.

There, on a mat in a house, I found the horribly mutilated
body of a fifteen-year-old girl. The neck was torn to ribbons
by the teeth and claws of the animal, the intestines were torn
out, the pelvis shattered, and one thigh was missing. A part of
the thigh, gnawed to the bone, and a piece of the shinbone lay
near the body. It seemed at first glance that only a beast of
prey could have treated the girl's body in this way, but closer
investigation brought certain peculiarities to light which did

not fit in with the picture. I observed, for example, that the skin at the edge of the undamaged part of the chest was torn by strangely regular gashes about an inch long. Also the liver had been removed from the body with a clean cut no beast could make. I was struck, too, by a piece of intestine the ends of which appeared to have been smoothly cut off, and lastly, there was the fracture of the thigh—a classic example of fracture by bending.

I had good enough reason now to share the doubts of the chief. To put the matter beyond any question I shot a monkey and threw it to my own two leopards. I could then observe with my own eyes that they did not tear their prey at all as the corpse I had to pronounce had been torn. In any case, dissection and study of the remains of the leopards' meal put it beyond any doubt that this was a case of a horrible murder committed by human hands in a way to suggest that the killer had been a leopard.

I drew up a report on my findings, and handed it to our highest police authority, the Mayor, who had recently been installed on the death of his predecessor. To make sure that he would not delay in giving the matter his active attention I gave him the report in person, although I never paid him a visit without extreme reluctance, because Liberian etiquette demanded that I should put on long trousers and a jacket for these official visits.

The new holder of this exalted office, unlike his rather casual predecessor, never permitted a European to visit him without turning the occasion into an official reception of the most portentous dignity. As a colonel in the Liberian Army and an aide-de-camp to the President, he thought he owed it to himself always to make his appearance in a theatrical pose which would have been more suited to a prince in comic opera. In my case, however, his gracious condescension was somewhat undermined by a bad conscience, for it probably occurred to him now and then that he had not paid me for my professional services and that I might be aware of the hollowness behind his splendid exterior. It was his habit every time he drank too much to send for me late at night, in a panic lest his last day had come. As his alcoholic excesses were very frequent, it is not surprising that one night I felt I had had enough of being roused up for no reason. So when I found him in bed, drunk as usual and surrounded by his wailing wives and concubines, I addressed him as follows:

"Colonel, there's no doubt about it. You have eaten or drunk something that hasn't agreed with you. Now if you like, I'll give you something which will get rid of it for you. It is a bit drastic—but certain."

I took his reply, "Oh, doctor, my friend, save me!" as permission to proceed, and I gave him a stiff dose of apomorphine (a powerful emetic), which without a moment's delay rid him of his poison so categorically that after that, however drunk he might be, he never again disturbed my rest.

A small incident showed that I had won his respect. I was had up for some trifle, and as I had no desire to waste time in a black court arguing the point, I sent the court messenger about his business with a quotation from a classical author. The court was furious when it received my reply, but the Colonel, who presided, recommended dismissing the case because the doctor could be very unpleasant when he lost his temper. After that I felt bound to write off his diplomacy as opportunism.

So now when he read the conclusions I drew from the post-mortem he was of course, as in duty bound, horrified, but not particularly eager to take action as head of the police. He regretted that my report, excellent as it might be, was of no interest to him; he knew all about that kind of murder. It was a secret society of the natives, the so-called Leopard Society, that initiated these murders at regular intervals. Unfortunately there was no protection against the scourge. But, for himself, he was not going out without a gun in his pocket in future. He wound up by congratulating me on my gifts as a detective, thanked me for my solicitude for the well-being of the inhabitants, and assured me of his support when ever I needed it.

That left things as they were, except that a cold panic spread through the native population. No one willingly stepped outside his door alone at night. Our postman to Sierra Leone refused to go on his long forest journey without the protection of two armed men, and on several occasions my nurses had to be severly reprimanded because they did not dare, even in emergencies, to fetch me from my house, which was eight or nine hundred yards from the hospital.

At last, when another leopard murder occurred in a distant village, they all breathed again, for now, so they said, there would not be another for a month. The "medicine" was satiated. But after three weeks their apprehension returned.

I could not understand how they all knew the rotation; nor could they themselves give me any precise explanation. They could only say they knew it from long experience and that the terror would continue as long as the dry season, with its parching heat, went on. Once the rains set in it would cease of itself.

Next a messenger came to me from the chief of Tosso summoning me to another post-mortem, and I went to the scene straight away in the motorboat.

This time it was an eight-year-old boy, and he had been mutilated in the same way as the girl of Tosso. There was again no doubt that it was murder, and probably the murderer was the same in each case.

The boy lived in the neighboring village of Jonni, where he attended the mission school, and had only been on a few days' visit to relations. His body was found in the forest, nearly a mile from the village, after he had been dead between one and two days. His relations and the Negro head of the mission school, Mr. Cane, who hastened to the scene, were inconsolable, and the whole village ran about like ants. Their terror that any one of them might be the next victim was pitiful. So, as I should never persuade the Colonel to take any steps in the matter, I decided to send my report on both cases direct to the Minister of the Interior in Monrovia.

To my complete amazement I received a very polite reply, which, however, left no doubt that further reports, or any interference on my part, were not desired. "In the interests of my personal safety" I was advised to keep right out of the matter in question.

I did not feel that I was in any danger. The "leopards" obviously confined themselves to children, and also I was a European. But for the time being, I could do nothing else but fall in with the Government's wishes.

My opinion of the courage of the murder gang was confirmed by their next victim, an old woman. As she was old and a freed slave, little notice was taken. Her time had pretty well come in any case.

It was the fifth murder, this time of an eighteen-year-old married woman, which brought the general agitation to boiling point. The chiefs of Tosso and Jonni, to whose territory the "leopards" had so far confined their atrocities, called for help, and the paramount chiefs of more distant territories feared lest the outbreak might spread. A deputation of chiefs therefore approached the Mayor and demanded heatedly that the Government should at last bestir itself.

The leader of the deputation was my very good friend the Gola chief, Boima Kui, and from him I heard what was said, and with what result.

The Colonel had once more shown himself a master of diplomacy. The assembled chiefs were overwhelmed with a torrent of fiery eloquence. He would crush the vermin with his armed fist. Had he not already stamped out this frightful Leopard Society in Bassaland with ruthless energy? And here too the miscreants should soon know with whom they had to deal. But first they had to be caught, and as they were concerned incontestably with a secret society of natives it would be very difficult, if not quite impossible, for him, an American Negro, to unmask the perpetrators. But something must be done without delay, and therefore he gave the following orders with effect from that moment:

1. A commission of three of the assembled chiefs to be set up under the presidency of the chief Boima Kui.

2. This commission to go at once to the neighborhood of Jonni, where most of the murders had taken place, and there remain, clothed with the fullest powers, until the perpetrators had been arrested.

3. For the credit of the country and the protection of the inhabitants the chiefs were to act with promptness, energy and decisive effect, or else themselves would be proceeded against with ruthless severity.

And now old Boima Kui was sitting on my veranda and drinking my beer with a rueful expression. He had expected a different result from the interview. Not that he was a coward. Far from it. Years ago, in the so-called Gola War, he had

212

made things awkward for the Government with his Gola warriors. But the prospect of being cooped up in Jonni, perhaps for months on end, if the Leopard Society did not meanwhile choose to show its hand, was no joy to him. He had no choice, however. Might he call on me at need? I said yes, by all means, and wished him good hunting.

For three weeks the luckless commission sat tight at Jonni and nothing happened. According to the gossip among the Negroes, the time was ripe for a new outrage, and my suspense became acute. So I arranged that my next routine visit to my outlying surgeries should take me through Jonni.

When I arrived there Boima Kui gave me a very hearty welcome. Naturally I had not forgotten to bring a few bottles of beer, and when his tongue was loosened and he began to feel benign and comfortable he told me the poor results of his efforts up to date. The commission had closely cross-examined numbers of persons, but even the usually "so reliable" methods of rolling sharp-edged rods of bamboo down the witnesses' shinbones had yielded very little. All the evidence was so confused that nothing could be made of it.

Then the fat Mambu, the village chief, came along accompanied by a small and aged native missionary named Cane, one of the few Negroes I have ever seen with almost white hair. Mambu made voluble excuses for not being able to find me accommodation in the village, as it was crowded with the chief's followers and all the people summoned to give evidence, but the old missionary Cane had vacated his own room for me at the mission outside. As I had brought my tent with me I needed no accommodation, but so as not to hurt the old boy I pitched it in his schoolyard. Although we slept under the aegis of the missionary, poor Massa nearly died of fright that night. He sat up beside my camp bed with the shotgun and a lighted

213

lamp, in full expectation of the Leopard-man, and probably wished his master to the devil a hundred times over.

Of course nothing happened except that Massa spent a sleepless night. And after the black priest had said mass and Boima Kui had ended his Mohammedan devotions, Massa and I set off for Jabacca, where we spent the day. Early the following morning a messenger came from Boima Kui with the surprising news that another murder had occurred that very night, and would I return at once.

This was really the height of audacity; they must feel very sure of themselves to strike under the very eyes of the commission.

Poor Massa—there was nothing for it, he had to go back with me. Before we even got to Jonni we met whole families fleeing from the accursed place with everything they possessed. They told us that a gigantic leopard had been in the village during the night and killed a man.

His death, at least, was confirmed when I got there. A young man of about twenty, an idiot, had spent the night in the hammock of a small open hut on the edge of the village. In the dead of night the village was roused by a frightful shrieking, which some described as the howling of a leopard, others as screams of a human being in the agony of death. Most of the inhabitants, in their terror, had barred their doors and windows, but the chiefs and a few stalwart men had armed themselves and hurried out. All they found was the young man, dead, close to his hammock with a broken neck.

The medical evidence was perplexing. The man had clearly been attacked in his hammock while asleep. On each side of his neck there were the marks of teeth, which might have been the teeth of a beast of prey. His neck was broken, but there were no other injuries.

Tracks of a leopard were distinctly visible on the floor of the hut and between the hut and the forest. What was surprising was that they were so confused that no exact conclusion could be drawn about the leopard's movements or its size.

I was in two minds myself whether this was not a case of a beast of prey, but Boima Kui had no doubts. In his view it was nothing but an insolent attempt to persuade the chiefs that a leopard was at work and that they might as well abandon their investigations. Without the slightest compunction he had sent for the nearest relatives of the dead man and begun by examining them. They had been sworn by secret magic and subjected to the shinbone torture. As this had not had the desired effect, the next day was appointed for the great magic of the wands.

I could not make out why he picked on the relatives of the dead man in particular for this brutal treatment, but I was not going to miss the "sasswood-palaver," or wand-magic, next morning.

The chiefs sat on their little carved seats in the palaver house, and in the open space in front sat a woman of about forty, fantastically gotten up. The inhabitants of the village made a wide circle round her and fixed upon her with awestruck eyes. Like most natives of her age, she was very thin and bony, but very muscular. Her neck was sinewy and her small head had an almost masculine look; her face was spare, ascetic looking, and deeply furrowed. Her large penetrating eyes were sunk deep in her head. She held a stout wand with both hands between her knees pointing down to the ground. Two other women squatted, one on each side of her, while in front of her, mute and resigned, stood a woman and four men, the relatives of the murdered man.

At a sign from Boima Kui one of the squatting women began

to tap on the witch's wand with a small rod in a slow and regular beat. The deathly stillness, so unlike a gathering in Africa, was in itself uncanny. The Negress stared at her wand, which she held towards the ground in stiffly outstretched arms. Slowly the steady beat of rod on wand grew quicker and quicker, and the arms and the whole body of the witch became more tense and rigid. She rolled her eyes and without relaxing her stiffened arms began to beat the ground with her wand in the same rhythm. As the tapping of the rod on the wand got louder, stronger, and faster, so did the tense beating of the wand on the ground. Convulsions ran through her rigid body; she fell over, writhing, and, without ceasing to beat the ground with her wand, jerked backward and forward in a deep hypnotic trance. The onlookers backed away in horrified alarm; even the five delinquents edged cautiously to the rear with wide and staring eyes. Then, as though the expected moment had come, the witch crouched and sprang on the woman who stood with the four men. She rained blows on her in an indescribable frenzy, like a mad woman, and at once her victim sank screaming to the earth; and the men leaped aside from her as from a serpent.

This crazy scene—the woman's screams, the pitiless blows, and the uproar that now burst out—were almost unbearable, but before I could overcome a paralyzing sense of horror and make up my mind what to do the wretched woman shouted something incomprehensible above the ceaseless thuds of the wand; whereupon some men instantly seized the furiously flagellating witch and tore her from her victim with surprising brutality. The two women who had originally supported her on each side held her by her wrists, loosened her clenched hands, and lowered her quivering body to the ground. There her trance gradually gave way and she lay utterly exhausted and apparently in a faint.

216

Meanwhile the woman who had been so shockingly beaten was quite as mercilessly dragged before the chiefs, to whom in terror and the wildest agitation she kept on shrieking over and over again, "It was I! I know it! Kill me!" That was all she could get out between her bloodcurdling shrieks.

I had had enough of this barbarous scene and was afraid I might still have to see an apparently innocent woman tortured to death. How could this weak woman have committed such a horrible murder?

And yet her guilt was clear. The charm was broken, and she betrayed one member after another of the Leopard Society, to which she too belonged. In turn they began to betray one another. In spite of lies and contradictions fresh facts were ascertained, and the commission was able at last to conclude its inquiry. About thirty members of the Leopard Society were taken and most of them confessed their guilt.

But the chief of this bloodthirsty band remained unknown. Perhaps those who were arrested did not themselves know him or perhaps he worked through intermediaries who had not been caught.

Long after the commission to its great relief had left Jonni, and when some of the prisoners, who were kept strictly guarded in a native hut, had already perished, fate played a strange trick. It put all the material evidence and the ringleader himself into the hands of the very man who had done least to free the people from the scourge. It was the Colonel, who, with his superior and condescending air, unmasked the ringleader before the eyes of the awed and respectful populace.

It happened thus:

One night a young man who had been setting traps in the forest near Jonni was overtaken by a violent thunderstorm and torrents of rain. As he was some way from the village he took shelter in a shed. It was not large, and it was cluttered up with

217

rubbish and boxes and tools. He was tired and the rain seemed endless, but there was no room to lie down. Then he saw that there were some boards and a mat laid across the beams which supported the sloping roof. Once up there he lay down to sleep.

Suddenly he was awakened by a noise. The door opened and a man came in with a small oil lamp which cast a dim light. He was obviously familiar with the place. The boy above was afraid to stir. From his hiding place he saw the man put down the lamp, open one of the large chests, take something out, and shut it again. But what he saw in the chest nearly froze the blood in his veins. He saw caps of leopard skin, claws of iron sheathed in leopard skin, spears, oddly shaped knives, and large pincers. All the implements of murder used by the Leopards were before his eyes, and that silent man with the lamp was without doubt their dreaded master.

His heart must have been pounding fit to burst until at last the door opened once more and the dark figure vanished with his lamp into the rain and darkness. Without a word to anyone he ran the fifteen miles from Jonni to Cape Mount next morning, driven on by panic, and told his story to the Mayor. The Mayor detained him and set some soldiers back to the hut in the forest.

Its owner, the old man with the lamp, the head of the Leopards, was taken, and the whole frightful business laid bare.

The doughty soldiers also arrested the black missionary, Cane, who offered no resistance. It was he who had brought this ancient and bloodthirsty religious order of the Leopards from his native Bassaland, south of Monrovia, and revived it in Cape Mount, where this kind of human sacrifice had for long been extinct. For it was a case of ritual murder, with its roots deep in the heathen mysticism of the natives.

218

The Master of the Leopards possessed a fetish from which issued a stronger magic than from any other "medicine." All who were within its magic circle had power over all who were not; it transformed them into leopards and exacted blood sacrifice.

What did this fetish look like? It was a lump of black wax about the size of a child's head, wrapped in cloths and bits of leopard skin. This dirty, greasy object was the great god who had devoured so many! Unfortunately I was not able to ascertain its exact composition, but judging from other smaller and less important magic agents, which I have been able to analyze it must have consisted of tightly bound leaves and various dried fragments of animal and vegetable origin. This kernel was the real heart of the magic; the thick wax covering was merely to protect it and to afford some sort of guarantee of the eternity of the magic power within.

Now if this magic lump was kept in a very dry place the wax inevitably began to dry up; and at the height of the dry season cracks appeared in its surface. This was the "medicine's call" for a sacrificial victim. The wax needed moisture; this explains the numerous murders in the dry season.

Some of the talismans required to be moistened with the blood of fowls or cattle or other creatures. But the mightiest, such as that of the Leopards, demanded human blood, and not merely human blood, but the blood of that member of the society on whom the choice of the talisman fell. This was the supreme sacrifice, and if a man by his blood could pass into the idol it followed that some of its supernatural power could pass into men. It was, however, impossible to sacrifice any large quantity of blood and survive. Consequently a logical way out was provided: I am not the only one of my blood, which runs also in the veins of my brothers and sisters, my mother and her brothers and sisters, and of their children. If I offer the blood of one of my blood relations I offer my own, and so the requirement of the god is met.

Boima Kui knew this, and that was why on the occasion of the last murder at Jonni he had come down at once and exclusively on the blood relations of the murdered youth.

All members of the society had to help the one who was the chosen sacrifice to procure the blood by means of ritual murder. They all worked themselves up to the wildest ecstasy by going through certain ceremonies and by drinking intoxicating and stupefying drinks, until they believed they were transformed into leopards. But some kept their heads clear enough to fall upon the selected victim, whom they murdered and carried off, leaving artificial leopard tracks. They then tore and mutilated their prey in an orgy of blood lust, imitating the wounds made by the claws and teeth of a leopard, and removing an organ containing blood. With this the wax covering of the precious object was saturated in a ceremony of peculiar solemnity. The cracks closed, and the "medicine" was satiated.

The idea of sacrifice when it first entered the mind of man, was certainly a noble one. The god, whose influence on mortal fate was dimly divined, was to share in mortal happiness. His blind power was to be invoked for the benefit of those who offered him what was precious to them; and the more precious the sacrifice the greater the benefits he would graciously confer. It was therefore only reasonable that Abraham should offer up his own blood, the blood of Isaac, his first-born son.

Human sacrifice can scarcely be regarded as a mere barbarous delusion. It was rather the final and highest outcome of the conception of sacrifice, of the aspiration of man to reach the stars. He sought in his distress to draw down divine help from the illimitable and mysterious universe and use it for his earthly needs. This is surely a tremendous thought, which found its fulfilment only when God himself, by the even greater sacrifice of His own Son, released the idea of sacrifice from its otherwise terrible consequences. Men were thus shown another way to God, the way of love, and the cruel slaughter of men and beasts had no further meaning. But even today the emotion aroused in us by the ideas of sacrifice and self-sacrifice show how strong a hold they must have had on the minds of our remote ancestors.

The trial of the false priest was an interesting and significant epilogue to the whole drama. His defense was conducted by his son, who lived in Cape Mount. It was perfectly simple and, in Liberian law, incontestable. He explained that his father had been received as a youth into the Society of Leopards and by the offering of his own blood had become identified with the leopard magic, and could never be separated from it, not even when he became a Christian. He was as innocent of the murders as all the other members of the society. As men, and in this case as Christians, they were, of course, incapable of such deeds, but when the magic power took hold of them they discarded their human form and became leopards. What they did after that was not done of their own will or by their own physical strength. As men they were innocent, and their guilt as leopards could not be assessed by any human court.

The court had not a word to say against such a conclusive argument. But to protect the people from further atrocities, and merely as a precaution, Mr. Cane was requested to leave the district. He retired to his native Bassaland, where he died two years later.

The Colonel too and Boima Kui and the old chief of Tosso have long since followed him.

CHAPTER 10

The Defeat of the Medicine Man

THE MONKS at Bolahun thought first of letting in the light of Christianity upon the centuries-old darkness of the primitive Negro soul; they asked little for themselves and gladly did without all the conveniences of civilized life. It was a very different matter with Father Simmonds, the progressive head of the mission station at Cape Mount. He wished the natives to have all the blessings of civilization as well as the Gospel. He himself stood with both feet firmly planted in the twentieth century, and every technical achievement of the age was a necessity to him. He was therefore my energetic supporter in my continual battle with the powers of the primeval forest—its gods and its laws and its almost insuperable resignation to what it took to be the inevitable. I had only to present an idea or an aim with the necessary perseverance and I could be sure that he would never rest until he had found the best and cheapest technical answer. His care of souls did not stand in the way of a technical ability that an expert might have envied. The pioneering spirit of his American forebears had come to life in him. Many a time I have seen him at work on a broken-down motor, covered in oil and sweat, and hurrying off next moment to wash and change just in time to take his service with the utmost devoutness.

Between the two of us, unaided but resolute, the virgin forest no longer had everything its own way. The battle was

222

exhausting and there were many setbacks, but each success brought us a little nearer our goal.

Simmonds' first triumph was electric light. The tropical day's twelve hours of light are too few, and the best of oil lamps are an endless annoyance. So a petrol engine was procured to supply us with current. Naturally it had to be treated like a film star lest it should leave us in the lurch. To get a spare part would have meant waiting for weeks in darkness.

Water was the next problem. We lived on the mountain-side, and relied for water on long trains of Negroes carrying up water in petrol tins on their heads from a spring below. In the rainy season there was a generous supply from above, which we collected in large tanks, and then the water carriers vanished from the scene. But with the dry season the daily two-way traffic was renewed.

Between the mission station and the hospital ran a gorge down which a stream rushed headlong all the year through. This stream we dammed with walls of cement, as high up the gorge as was practicable, to make a small reservoir out of which two large pipes led to two plunger pumps lower down the hill-side. These pumps pumped part of the water up into water tanks placed at a height above our settlement. The natives wagged their heads at the white man's magic which stamped night and day and made water flow uphill. Water was laid on from our water tower to all the buildings, and now they had to believe the fairly tales Massa had brought back with him from Germany about water coming out of a wall when you turned a door handle.

But what headaches, sweat, and worry our engineering cost us until at last water, clear, good, and irreproachable, flowed from the taps!

We had scarcely congratulated ourselves on the success of

our waterworks before they automatically introduced a further problem. The hygienic disposal of the waste water was urgent; so too was the unpleasant question of sewage. Our aim was the orthodox water closet. While Simmonds was kept busy repairing a defect in the reservoir, I made use of my European leave to go as apprentice to a sanitary engineer after two months at a clinic, where I took a refresher course in medicine.

He was a stout and worthy master craftsman, who was amused at taking on his long, lean, academic pupil. When I felt I had mastered the rudiments and said good-by to him he shook me vigorously by the hand: "Now doctor, when back in Africa you have pulled the chain for the first time and are rewarded by a fine flush of water, do please send me a post card."

I did better. In my joy I went as far as a cable. "It flushes stop doctor stop."

But as usual, the mere installation was the simplest part. The mistakes we made did not show up until later. Either the waste pipes got blocked, or the three-chambered settling pond collapsed with a horrid roar, or the filtering plant choked the outlet in the reservoir and the automatic pump gave up. Then the good Father was kept on the run with his native engineers until the fault was detected and the damage repaired. The lessons of experience were hard, but our native apprentices learned as well as we ourselves, and they began to acquire a technical insight into what they had taken for magic.

There was still another problem awaiting a solution. I have mentioned already that the hospital and my house were separated by about eight hundred yards and that the Negro nurses were often afraid to fetch me at night when I was urgently needed, because the path skirted the edge of the forest. So I got some old telephone apparatus and ran a line to the hospital.

The Defeat of the Medicine Man

For the sake of simplicity I wound the wire on to broken-off necks of beer bottles, which were stuck on to the branches of trees. After a violent storm I distributed a few new beer bottle necks, and the natives set about mending my "talking clothes-line" with the greatest enthusiasm.

Step by step we learned how to build more modern and practical houses, with better roofs than the hot and noisy corrugated iron. We also made good use of the plentiful and beautiful wood for furniture of improved design. The days of cooling my drinks in damp cloths and of perforating a tin-box to make my first shower bath were long past. Our well-run houses had no trace now of the primitive conditions of the virgin forest. Refrigerator, telephone, radio—all were at our command. We lacked nothing that makes civilized life tolerable—or intolerable.

It was only when we went on trek that the forest took command again and imposed on us the train of porters and the nights in native huts.

One of the chief sufferings, if one was not disposed to do the whole journey on foot, was traveling in a hammock, the usual vehicle of the white man. But for the first time the priest and the doctor were unable to see eye to eye when this problem of conveyance came up for discussion.

Simmonds built a ricksha out of old bicycles while I thundered through the forest on a motorcycle. Naturally, each of us favored his own conveyance, but both of them had their drawbacks. The ricksha was comfortable, but slow, and dependent on one coolie instead of on two porters. Besides this, the forest tracks were often too narrow for it, and sometimes one wheel sank in a morass. With my motorcycle, journeys of days were done in hours. I had my baggage in a small trailer and was quite independent; but the trailer shared the fate of

225

the ricksha: it was often too wide for the track, and then both I and it went over. Thick roots often crossed the narrow paths, forcing me either to get off or to come off; and then there were the tree trunk bridges, over which I had to coax the cycle all on my own. In fact, neither means of conveyance was perfect, and they were rivals to the end.

We had ordered a Klepper tent, and this made us independent of native huts. Zip-fastening secured us against driver ants and snakes by night, and a curtain of mosquito net against mosquitoes and flies by day. Ample ventilation, folding camp furniture, and air mattresses provided adequate comfort, and we could now travel on wheels through the forest and spend the night where we pleased.

But above all, the motorboat, ricksha, and motorcycle brought the inland regions nearer. There were no longer those exhausting weeks of journeying on foot or by canoe when we wanted to visit villages of the Vais and Golas. It was easier to get there, and we could go more often. We also made our way to places never visited hitherto.

Now at last my efforts to give the natives medical care and above all instruction in hygiene had some partial success. I could show them there and then, in their own surroundings, what sins they habitually committed and how necessary it was to stamp out the sources of infection.

It was not a simple matter in most cases to overcome their ancient customs and habits and the deadening influence of the medicine man. Do what I would, I utterly failed to get on to a friendly footing with these gentlemen, as I had done at Bolahun. From the start they were my bitter enemies, because instead of confining myself to Cape Mount I went out of my way to invade the Negro village, their own inalienable domain. They did all they could to drive me from the field. Secret designs of destroying the whole race and other absurdities were foisted on me; the sick were warned and frightened; and while my successes were made little of, or else denied, their own were loudly proclaimed.

To have aroused the deadly enmity of this powerful black brotherhood was a serious matter. I had my clearest proof of this when I introduced the new treatment of gonorrhea with sulphonamide.

The increase of this disease among the natives was phenomenal, and very few had the patience for the prolonged treatment hitherto in force; and so the brief and simple treatment with sulphonamide was a true deliverance for both patient and doctor. Yet suddenly the stream of patients was cut off. The reason was that the black magicians had pronounced that although the new medicine was a cure for gonorrhea, it left the patient sterile. This hit the Negro, with his great longing for progeny, in his tenderest place. I might deny it as often and as emphatically as I liked—it was no use. I had to wait nine months, as least, until Nature could give the lie to it on her own account. Until then I was left with the best cure the world then had to offer on my hands. There were no takers.

Is it surprising after this that I was seized with a holy rage against such infamous malice on the part of my black colleagues? Whenever I encountered one of the fraternity I went straight for him with the deliberate intention of making him look a fool.

Not much came of these arguments as a rule; but once I had a shattering success. I arrived at Jenne-Wunde just as the medicine man, with some difficulty, had made a boy bring up something which had disagreed with him. The District Commissioner, who was there by chance, the chief, and all the people were filled with amazement. I smiled scornfully at such a wonderful exhibition, and said that what he did with deluges of salt water, I could do in a moment with the mere prick of a needle. I was thinking of my experiences with the Mayor, Colonel Davis, in his drunken bouts, and hoped I might have the chance of repeating the well-attested cure. To my great joy the medicine man declared that nothing of the sort could occur with him, as his magic was the stronger. Now I had him where I wanted him and proposed to make the trial.

The Negroes were in the wildest excitement at the prospect of a duel between the white medicine man and the black, and the District Commissioner too soared to a great height of enthusiasm. My black colleague had to accept the challenge now or else be damned for ever. He had walked into the trap with his eyes open. We all repaired to the palaver house, and the District Commissioner declared himself umpire, while the two contestants tried their weapons. The magician anointed himself with an ointment of some sort, bound an armlet to each arm and each leg, and I produced a ampoule of my trusty apomorphine. I then gave him the injection, to which he submitted without a tremor. Confident of victory, I lit a cigarette and sat down. There was dead silence, and all eyes were fixed first on the white doctor, then on the black. God, if it did not come off? I should be finished for good and all! My opponent sat stock still on the ground, as though in a trance. And yet I seemed to see a grayish tinge spreading over his face.

A few minutes more and he was clearly becoming restless. The audience too observed that a crisis was approaching.

My courage returned, and to heighten the dramatic effect I stood up and announced that the moment had come. "You will soon see him vomit now."

This broke down the last barrier. He sprang up and tried to leave the palaver house, but the District Commissioner called out to his soldiers standing among the crowd: "Don't let him go! He has to stay here!"

At that my defeated opponent flung himself on the ground, and what had to come, came. The people, who had loudly acclaimed him a few minutes before, now shouted with laughter and made him drink the bitterness of defeat to the dregs. I was honestly sorry for the man when I saw him writhing on the ground and heard his groans. But I could not relent, for more was at stake than this one man—namely, the power of helping thousands of sick people. For their sake his defeat had to be decisive.

I went to see him in his hut after the event and tried to console him with a present of money. It was useless. I am even convinced that he and his guild of medicine endeavored to get rid of me by many a secret sorcery. But that was no good either.

An emetic had cleared my path. Now I had to make the most of my opportunity. I had to establish myself and my medicine in the forest, for it would be too much to expect the natives to take my side altogether. They were at bottom too conservative, and nothing but an uninterrupted flow of cures would ever convince them.

I had to occupy and hold every inch I could wrest from the forest and its ancient superstitions, and so I built small surgeries in the native style at Mambu, Damballa, and Baigbong, each of which was put in charge of a fully trained and resident nurse. Injections for the yaws could be given in these surgeries; malaria, dysentery, and the various diseases due to worms treated, and ulcers bandaged. Two beds were provided for clinical cases and confinements. Infant welfare and the carrying out of hygienic instructions could also be supervised. Patients released from the Cape Mount hospital could be given aftercare and many a toilsome journey to the doctor spared them.

Once such surgeries were established they were mostly self-supporting. The only difficulty was the initial outlay. But here the American journals devoted to good works came to our aid. They made our needs known, and I soon found patrons who undertook to pay the cost of building each of my surgeries and who also came to their help in case of need. To keep them interested we sent them photographs of the hospitals which bore their names and also monthly reports with a detailed financial statement.

The next thing was to establish a regular courier service to keep me in closer touch with these upcountry surgeries than my frequent personal visits could do. These couriers took out medical apparatus and drugs, provisions, paraffin for the lamps, and so on, and brought back to the mother-hospital patients and samples for analysis, so that medical problems could be speedily solved in spite of the distance.

A considerable part of the primeval forest was thus covered with a network of medical outposts, which for the first time disputed its immemorial sway. It was even planned to organize a motorboat service up the more important rivers for the transport of lepers to the island of Massateen, but unfortunately this was never carried out.

There was, however, such a service by ocean-going yacht between Monrovia and Cape Mount, conveying sick persons who wished to consult me. It arrived once a week with a cargo of sick, and took back the cured. As this traffic was mostly in well-off and civilized Negroes, it grew to such a pitch that only a new and more up-to-date hospital could possibly cope with it. After I had written a long article explaining the need for this,

The Defeat of the Medicine Man

I discovered to my great joy that the money for endowing just such a scheme was already available in America.

But before it could be put at my disposal I was to await the visit of an elderly lady, the president of an important American charitable organization, who was to decide whether this was a suitable way of applying the endowment.

Nothing therefore was left undone to give this lady the best possible impression of our work at Cape Mount. The hospital was put into curling papers, the patients turned into Adonises, and hours were spent in selecting the most comfortable mattress for our important guest. We did all that was humanly possible to ensure her a pleasant visit, but there was one thing we could not influence, and that was the sea. Now, unfortunately, was the very time when the reef became impassable, and passengers had to be put ashore by boat on the beach of the long promontory. We could only hope that Neptune would show some sense of decency on this great occasion.

Punctually at five o'clock in the afternoon in question, the smart white yacht of the Bishop of Monrovia rounded the Cape and dropped anchor on the reef. All the American missionaries, and all the schoolmistresses, all my family and I hastened down the mountain side to receive our honored guest in person —what won't one do for money!

When we got to the beach we found to our consternation that the rough sea and the wall of surf made it impossible to launch a boat of any size. So there we stood surrounded by a small gathering of inquisitive natives, gazing helplessly out to sea, where the yacht tossed up and down and tugged wildly at her anchor.

What was to be done? Not for the world could I let this lady sail away again. I was counting on the money. I could not hail her; the distance was too great and the sea too loud.

But I had to do something besides waving like a fool. Someone had to get to her, and that someone had to be—me. So I turned to the chief of the Kru Negroes, who deal with all sea-going matters, and told him to get me a seaworthy canoe and two experienced men to row it. A long palaver followed. I was like a cat on hot bricks, expecting every moment to see the yacht raise anchor and set sail.

At last the chief came up to me with a stout fisherman. "This is the only man who will go. The others say the sea is too rough."

"Right." I said. "Then off we go!"

But there was more to it than that.

"What will you pay, *loketa?*"

Money again, always money! But there was more money than this at stake, so I replied recklessly, "A shilling!"

Another long, nerve-wracking powwow followed. At last the chief gave me the result. "My brother says to put out now is a matter of life and death. If he dies his wife will have nothing to eat. And if he risks his life at my word, then I shall have to pay for it."

This was in all conscience a wild exaggeration. The fellow could for certain swim like a fish and, anyway. I could not fix him up with a life insurance policy at that time of day. "Five shillings for his life, then," I burst out. "But on condition we get off right now."

"Thank you, *loketa,* you are indeed a very good man. My brother will go at once and fetch his paddles," the old man replied.

Fetch his paddles—it was enough to drive me mad! And suppose my dollar-princess made off meanwhile! To put the interval to good use I exchanged the long white trousers I had put on in honor of the occasion for Father Simmonds's khaki shorts. They were a yard too wide, but better for swimming in, and swim I should have to before long. As I happened at that time to have horrible tropical ulcers on both legs, which were swathed in bandages, I did not gain much in outward appearance by the exchange. My consolation was that Father Simmonds, who was short and fat, did not at all look the part of president of a reception committee, in white trousers far too tight and far too long for him. But what did anything matter so long as she did not set sail?

The paddles arrived and we started. Watched by the respectful throng, we pulled a long, narrow, shell-like dugout down to the sea and took up our stations on each side of it, leaning forward like runners before the start of a race, our hands resting on the boat, I at the bow and the Negro at the stern. Above on the beach the old Kru chief kept a sharp watch on the breakers as they rolled in, waiting for a momentary lull.

"Wait, wait—now!"

At the word we rushed into the water, with the boat gripped between us.

"In!" the boy shouted, and he was in already, but I was not quite so fast. It is not such a simple matter when you're up to your waist in water to leap nimbly into a cockleshell of a canoe. But once in I seized my paddle and dug furiously into the water. That, at least, was my intention. But the sea crashed in on top of me. We were in the ditch!

When I came to the surface I just had the chance to take a breath before the boat caught me a crack on the head, smashed my helmet down over my eyes, and away I went again.

Next a wave shot me on to the hard beach like a stone from a sling. There lay the boat, and there my paddle, and there, with a grin on his face, stood my black companion.

So much for that, and now for a second attempt. I abandoned my helmet this time and resolved to be even quicker than before.

Again we waited for the old man's signal. Again we dashed up to our middles into the water, and I jumped with some approach to agility into the canoe. I held my paddle in a grip of iron and went to work with all I had.

"Hard, *loketa,* faster, faster!" my boy commanded.

A gigantic wave approached, and our bow skewered it right in the middle. I knew no more. I only felt that I must have taken one direction and the boat another, for I sat on nothing. Next, I was spinning round and round, gasping for breath at intervals, until in the same graceful parabola as before, I landed on the beach. My boy, the boat, and the paddle were waiting for me.

My wife thought I had now given proof enough of my prowess on the sea, but I wanted to make one more attempt; and, as ever, obstinacy was rewarded. The canoe, the boy, and I got through the surf in one piece. Certainly our dugout was full to the gunwale, and we scarcely dared move for fear of capsizing. But, while we bobbed about on the swell, we very cautiously baled with our hands and also by means of kicking in time with our feet, until it was safe to paddle again.

All the time we drew near to the anchored yacht I kept my eyes on an elderly lady with gray hair who was seated aft in a deck chair, watching as through a telescope. I quickly smoothed back my wet hair, which was hanging down over my face; the impression I was bound to make on this important person was bad enough without that. I was wet through; I was in shorts; I was swathed like a Laocoön in the bandages which now uncovered my hideous wounds; and of course I was barefoot. As for the bruise on my nose which the boat had given me at our first attempt, of that, at least, I was blissfully ignorant until I got home.

With the help of the Negro crew I swung myself on board the rolling and pitching yacht and stood like a castaway fished dripping from the sea.

"Welcome to Cape Mount! I am the doctor."

A right royal welcome to my guest, I thought. But the lady did not seem to be overcome, and replied with a polite, "Glad to meet you, Doctor. Take a seat, will you?"

Her gray eyes looked at me sharply and questioningly through her spectacles, but she said no more. It was for me, I felt, to say something. But what was I to say next? If only I could get her ashore! That endowment—a thousand thoughts chased through my head, and among them all I came out with the silliest one I could have chosen: "Can you swim?"

"Swim? Do you take me for a mermaid? You don't suppose *I'd* sit on that bit of wood and ride ashore like that?"

"No, of course not," I hurriedly assured her. "I was just—asking."

To this even sillier remark she replied with a curt, "I see."

The time had come to say something rather more to the point. If she had only offered me a cigarette, but she sat rigid and erect in her chair, as though our interview might continue in this manner for hours.

"We shall have to wait until the sea calms down before you can come ashore." That was better, and I bravely went on. "It may take some time, but there is no need to give up and go back to Monrovia."

"I should say not," she replied. "I haven't come to Cape Mount in order to go back with the job undone. I shall land whatever happens."

She took a ton-load off my mind. The money was safe. And

now I could venture to give her a preview of what the future had in store. "In half an hour it will be dark, and it will be early morning at the soonest before the sea is any calmer. Naturally I shall remain here on board with you until then."

To this she replied without a change of expression and in the same tone of command.

"Young man, you will do nothing of the kind. What would your wife say to your remaining all night on board with me? I can very well stay here alone till morning."

I might have asked her what she thought my wife would say. Instead I inquired sympathetically whether she would not be seasick, tossing at anchor all night.

"No, I certainly shall not, for the very good reason that I have been seasick already for the last three hours to a degree I have never before experienced in all my many voyages. And now you can go, my dear doctor. I shall hope to land tomorrow morning in calm weather, and I shall hope also that your kind wife will have a good cup of coffee ready for me."

There was something almost human about that, and admiration for her courage and composure, in spite of seasickness and my inane remarks, warmed my parting counsels for the night. Then, after a display of gymnastics, I managed to get back into the canoe.

The plan for our return journey was for us to be carried ashore, like surf riders, on the crest of a wave; so we again waited for the old man's signal, and then paddled for all we were worth. But paddle as we might we slowly fell away from the wave's heaving shoulders, and soon we lay in a deep trough at the mercy of the next one. This brought upon us a repetition of what we had survived twice already, except that this time the boy took to the water first. Then we were both flung with violence at the feet of the committee waiting on the beach.

The Defeat of the Medicine Man

Next morning, just before six, our guest appeared unannounced at our door. After a night of agony she had gotten ashore dry-shod in a calm sea. We quickly succumbed to her superb sense of humor and her heart of gold, of which she gave one more proof in the benefaction made to the hospital. But when she returned to Monrovia it was by land.

A feverish time at the drawing board now set in. I could spend 100,000 dollars in building a hospital to my own design without being accountable to anybody. All that our American benefactors asked was that this sum should not be exceeded. They had the very unusual but very sensible idea that I knew best what I wanted, and so left me a free hand in carrying it out.

I went to Germany, discussed my sketch and ground plan with an architect, bought all the building materials, and then the great work of building began. Apart from a few quite useful native masons, who could at least use a spirit level even if they did not always do so, we had no skilled craftsmen. So Simmonds and I had to superintend every detail in person, and too often we had to knock down in a fury at night what our bricklayers had built askew during the day. The ground plan, which was in the form of an E, with long projecting wings, was particularly troublesome. When we discovered that the foundation walls, instead of remaining parallel, were three-quarters of a yard or more out, there was nothing for it but to bend them gradually inward. This device succeeded very well and was never noticed.

As the site cost us nothing we could build spaciously on one floor only, and in order to defeat the ever-present termite no wood at all was used. Doors and windows were of steel and glass, the roof of iron girders and asbestos tiles. On paper it all looked simple enough, but we often tore our hair when it came to carrying it out. Owing to the curvature of the walls we found that the girders cut to length on the ground were too short in places; a third of the tiles had been broken while they were being landed in a rough sea; the elaborate plumbing required in a hospital taxed us sorely; and then we found that owing to a miscalculation we were short of several sockets and flanges, so the job was held up until we could procure these missing parts from Europe. The roofing of the octagonal operating theater, which projected from the main building, was achieved only at the fifth attempt, when we were on the verge of despair. Finally, a kapok tree, cut down too late, fell the wrong way and destroyed some of our masonry. Every day after my work at the old hospital I set off in fear and trembling to discover what was the latest to go wrong with the new one.

My wife had as much trouble with the accounts as we had with the building. Items in five different currencies had to be entered in one account, and leaves of tobacco, native "irons," and American coppers had to be estimated at their current value. The English shilling was the principal currency in Liberia, and so whole sacks of silver had to be kept in our treasury and counted for literally hours on end.

It took a year and a half before the hospital I had dreamed of and longed for was there before my eyes. At last I had a workshop which met all the up-to-date demands of a tropical hospital and in which the equipment down to the last detail was all brand-new. The most modern, cool, steel furniture had been supplied from Germany and above all I now had an X-ray apparatus, the need for which I had felt so bitterly.

Our Mayor, the Colonel, in top hat and morning coat, and wearing his decorations, was present at the opening, together with representatives of the Government, all the leading chiefs, and the whole town in its smartest clothes. Afterwards the hospital was thrown open to the closest inspection; and what aroused the greatest admiration was not the admittedly somewhat mysterious X-ray apparatus, but, very surprisingly, the operating table, which could be slanted and fixed at all angles.

A great spread, with the usual speeches, dancing, and devil dances, followed, and the ceremony became in the end a regular festival.

In addition to my daily hospital duties, my responsibilities as Medical Officer for Health for the whole province, my leper settlement on Massateen, the outlying surgeries, and the ever-increasing flow of patients from the capital, I now had sixty hospital beds to reckon with.

All this meant that the work was rather too much for me to carry on single-handed, and I was very glad when the German Research Fellowship put three doctors a year at my disposal to gain experience in tropical medicine. My task was now a light one. And besides this the yearly change of assistants brought a continuous flow of new life, from which our situation cut us off. The ensuing battle with the Government of Liberia was also not without its attraction.

Dr. Fuszeck, Minister of Health, did not wish to see a medical center of gravity at Cape Mount; quite enough metropolitan sufferers repaired there already. Also the Government had a fear of spies, which at that time was perhaps understandable, although in this case quite groundless. Consequently the employment of German doctors was unconditionally forbidden me; then on my intercession it was allowed again, and then yet once more it was forbidden, until these protracted negotiations eventually ended in a compromise. One German assistant was permitted; the others had to be of some other nationality. For some odd reason this solution was accepted as a guarantee that

Cape Mount would not become a center either of medical activity or of dreaded espionage.

In any case, I had my helpers and therefore the opportunity to devote myself to still wider activities.

The establishment of the upcountry surgeries had shown the lack of an adequate reserve of trained nursing staff. I therefore started a school for nurses and orderlies with the co-operation of my American patron. Girls and young men who had passed through State or mission schools were admitted. After a three-year course they were given a certificate as nurses or orderlies, and since this was recognized by the State they could work anywhere in the country. I kept the best of them back for advanced training as operating theater nurses, chemists, and laboratory assistants. Others specialized in hospital management and midwifery.

Midwifery was the branch in which I had taken a very particular interest ever since I became more closely acquainted with the way it was practiced among the natives. I had no such opportunity in my first years in Africa. For a doctor—that is, a man—to take any part in childbirth was utterly contrary to native ideas. Even the black medicine man kept entirely aloof from all such matters.

The chief midwife is the mistress of the Bundu, the women's secret society, and all problems arising out of childbirth are her responsibility alone. She is the guardian of morals and sees to it that the traditional code of feminine modesty and behavior is strictly observed. As midwife she has the women in her power in their gravest need, and since all Negro women know that she exacts a full confession before delivering them, they are very careful at all times not to incur her anger. For some of the laws are of draconian severity. Among the Buszis, for example, it is death for any woman if she allows a man in any circumstances to see her genital organs, a law which rules out gynecology from the start. The explanation is not simply that the Bush-mistress likes to exercise authority in moral matters; she is also opposing the all-powerful Gri-gri Bush of the men and its magic rites. She has a realm of equal power based on an exclusively female concern. By this means her power is increased and also her emoluments in the form of propitiatory offerings for small offenses, wheedled by the women out of their husbands.

When a woman thinks she is pregnant she goes to the midwife, who after confirming the fact gives her precise instructions and looks after her during the pregnancy. The choice of a concubine for her husband is also discussed, unless of course he has several women in his household already; appropriate offerings are presented, and the whole course of life prescribed. When the time approaches the midwife and a few experienced women take the woman into the forest. There they all squat on mats, and when labor commences, the woman, if she wants to have an easy delivery, must make full confession of all her sins. If she wearies in her labor, two of the women press with all their weight on her body and beat it with their fists, in order to arouse the birth pangs and to make the woman exert pressure too; or else they bind a cloth lightly round her and roll it downward. If all else fails, the wretched woman is firmly held from behind by one of the crouching women; the midwife, facing her, forces her knees apart while two other of the women brutally pound her body. In consequence of the injury done in the early initiation rites, the channel is often unyielding and severely torn. As soon as the child is successfully born the midwife bites or breaks off the navel string, and the child is rubbed with palm oil and wrapped in some old rags. Complications caused by withholding of the afterbirth are surprisingly frequent and much dreaded, and so the birth is no sooner over than the squeezing and pommeling begins over again, combined with tugging at the navel string. When all is over the woman is allowed a little rest and then taken secretly back to her house. If a woman dies in childbirth it means that she has concealed some offense committed against the laws of the Bundu society. Nevertheless she counts as one killed in battle. All the women of the village assemble, the Bush-mistress and her confederates borrow swords and other weapons, and announce the news with wild war songs and brandishing of swords and clamor, while the dead woman is buried in secrecy and silence.

Among the Negroes and most primitive races, childbirth, which is, after all, a natural function, passes off in the great majority of cases without complications; yet I had come across many instances of grave harm being done by their wrong ideas of midwifery. But every effort I made, even through my trained native nurses, to get a footing in this sphere was in vain, until at last my old friend the chief of Tosso village took the law into his own hands and brought his wife, who was on the verge of death, straight to the hospital. I succeeded in saving the mother's life at least, and the ban was broken. Secretly at first, and openly later on, difficult cases were brought to me, often at the cost of a day's journey. I then saw cases which were often lamentable indeed, and each time I was filled with deeper regret that I was unable to exercise a stronger influence on the midwives. At last the long desired fruit of my labors fell into my lap without any direct intervention on my part.

A civilized Liberian woman consulted me for pains in the abdomen. I found a tumor of the size of a child's head in the lower abdomen and advised an operation. But she said that the native midwife had declared that she was pregnant and that therefore she must not be operated on. I tried to convince them of the error, but had no success. A few months later the woman was brought to me again, this time in a desperate state. In spite of the sick woman's protests, the midwife had declared that her time had come, and had put her through the whole process of a native delivery. As the tumor showed no disposition to be "born" in the natural way, the woman had been pommeled and beaten and at last pushed down again and again with her pelvis against the edge of a large rice mortar, until she had broken down under the injuries inflicted.

She then brought a charge of attempted murder against the midwife. In the course of the trial I obtained, almost as a matter of course, the promulgation of a law that all births must take place in the hospital until every native midwife had been passed by me as competent.

From then on I always had three or four of these Bush-mistresses in the hospital, and they had to be present at all births which took place under our supervision. I pride myself on having won the confidence of every one of them, in spite of the lofty airs they put on at first and their very reluctant co-operation. It was a very comic sight when these dirty old bush-Negresses had to wash themselves and put on white aprons in a spotless modern hospital; but in the end they were really grateful, and for the future sent all abnormal cases to the hospital of their own accord and in good time. Probably at the bottom of their hearts they felt the relief of being able to shelve the responsibility for difficult cases, even though their power over the women, who now often came straight to us to have their children, was somewhat weakened.

Then later on when we sent our nurses trained in midwifery at the hospital to work in the villages, the old Bush-mistresses were smart enough to get them into the Bundu Bush and leave childbirths to them. They, however, remained the great ladies, and thus I attained by peaceful means what had cost me hard battles in the case of the medicine men.

It was a far easier task to bring my influence to bear on the shockingly high rate of infant mortality, which had always been a weight on my mind. I began by arranging talks for mother and child on Sunday evenings, when I gave the mother practical advice in the care of infants. Free medicines for the children and prizes for the mothers of well cared for children were available from charitable funds. Each child was given a card on which each attendance at these talks was entered. When a mother had kept her child in good health for six months, or at least brought it regularly for inspection, she received a substantial reward in baby clothes, linen, and such. The aim was to tempt the women to bring their children even when healthy, and so benefit by instruction. We hoped in this way to free the whole question of the rearing of children from irrational superstitions and to save many young lives.

Advice to mothers was also given in our outlying surgeries, and what the women most looked forward to was the half-yearly baby shows in which the doctor took part. A whole English pound, a real fortune for a Negress, was the dazzling first prize for the healthiest and best kept baby. It was not easy for us to pick out the winner from among dozens of naked, fat-tummied babies, all howling lustily, without being well scratched by the unsuccessful mothers.

It showed them that there was something to gain from listening to us and following our instructions. We wanted them to understand that if their children died it was not just magic or fate, but lack of proper care or wrong feeding. I could not, of course, abolish malaria, which was endemic and the chief cause of death among children. But I could at least make sure that they were strong and healthy enough to withstand it when they first got infected.

It was a long and weary task to disabuse the natives of their traditional ideas and notions about sickness and its causes, and to implant in them by degrees entirely novel ones, which to us are second nature; and of course it was impossible to visit every village and give lectures. So I gave boys from the mission schools practical instruction, illustrated my material from the hospital laboratory. They took to this more enthusiastically than to the Gospel and three-times-three. In the holidays they went back to their villages bursting with knowledge, and also with contempt for the ignoramuses there, who promptly believed all that the boys told them. When a father has lived the primitive life of the native it does not always strike him as odd that his small son knows things that he does not. It is a voice from another world speaking to him through his son, and even though he may not understand much, and may not wish to, in some way he pays attention; and if he finds that he is freed from sickness and the dread of evil spirits he is often, owing to his greater experience of life, more obedient to what his children say than they ever were to him.

All the same, if I wanted to banish from their minds their belief in magic, at least in my own sphere of medicine, I had to beware of believing in magical results; my helpers and I could not in a few years turn the primitive Negro into a representative of the twentieth century. But such success as we had was seen in our patients.

The long and woeful queue of sufferers who had dragged their loads of misery year after year gradually disappeared. The time when women with tumors weighing fifty pounds, and men with gargantuan forms of elephantiasis came to us in the last stages of desperation was over. Early cases were now increasingly in the majority. This could be put down only to our long battle, and this success brought another with it. For when our patients came to us in good time the proportion of cures went up.

We were deluded only in believing that the work would be any lighter. Our successes added to the demands made upon us, for the sick were not now content merely to be rescued in extremity; they came to us for medical attention of the most expert and specialized kinds.

Our triumph was demonstrated when, after we had success-fully replaced a nose with a plastic substitute and also cured a severe hysterical paralysis by hypnotism, an old black medi-cine man who for years had run his rival show at the foot of the hospital hill shut up shop. "This man don't know nothing. He's old-fashioned," was the verdict of the people; and it was a moral death sentence for him and his like. This was precisely what I had been striving for. It was for them to see for them-selves that their ideas of sickness and magic and enchantment were old-fashioned. The tyranny which the primeval forest and the black medicine men exercised over their souls and bodies had to be broken.

When they themselves saw this my aim was achieved. And once it happened in the sphere of medicine the chains which bound them to their Iron Age were loosened, and they were ready for the spiritual liberty offered by the missionary and the teacher.

I have often wondered whether the battle against all that the primeval forest meant, and the inculcation of progress, were the right thing for these primitive savages. Perhaps they lived more happily and peaceably in their own world with their own beliefs and notions, even if they included the perpetual fear of magic and its derivatives such as the Leopard Society.

The Defeat of the Medicine Man

Was it not worse to be awakened than to dream on in the green twilight of the forest?

But was the dream so great a blessing? And if it was, had not the awakening inevitably come? Had not the white man, in his urgent pursuit of gain, already roused the natives from sleep and flung them into an alien world?

He had implanted in them needs hitherto unknown, brought on them the compulsion of wage earning, and an economy tied to capital. New diseases and vices, and the example of moral hypocrisy and worthlessness, had been introduced by the less worthy representatives of civilization. Misunderstanding and arrogant superiority had classed them as mere tools which were needed for the economic exploitation of Africa.

In the face of this irresistible development, by which the whole native way of life was necessarily destroyed, it was surely superfluous to have scruples about giving them new ideals. Now that he was inevitably embarked on the stormy seas of the twentieth century, the least that could be done in fairness was to teach the native the most valuable lessons of Christianity, technical science, and medicine.

Anyone who admits this and has dedicated his life to the service of others must think himself fortunate if he has been able to improve the lot of these unfortunate Negroes, even if only as a white medicine man in the primeval forest.

The hammer blows of the Second World War smashed the fabric of so many hopes and dreams.

Once again the white man showed how little he was able to follow his own counsels of brotherly love and mutual understanding, and the native looked on in open-eyed surprise.

I was able to keep the hospital running until the spring of 1940, and then I had to return to Germany with my family by tortuous paths. My last assistant, Dr. Kock-Grünberg, left the country too in 1941.

The upcountry surgeries closed their doors, the elephant grass grew over the ruins on Massateen, and the new hospital stood as a sole monument to past glories, but also as a starting point for the work of a new doctor in days to come.

May he never lose sight of what alone is the making of life out there—faith in the ultimate victory of goodness among men!